Bending the Cost Curve

Solutions to Expand the Supply of Affordable Rentals

About the Urban Land Institute

The mission of the Urban Land Institute is to provide leadership in the responsible use of land and in creating and sustaining thriving communities worldwide. Established in 1936, the Institute today has more than 30,000 members worldwide, representing the entire spectrum of the land use and development disciplines. ULI relies heavily on the experience of its members. It is through member involvement and information resources that ULI has been able to set standards of excellence in development practice. The Institute has long been recognized as one of the world's most respected and widely quoted sources of objective information on urban planning, growth, and development.

About the ULI Terwilliger Center for Housing

The mission of the ULI Terwilliger Center for Housing is to expand housing opportunity by leveraging the private sector and other partners to create and sustain mixed-income, mixed-use urban and suburban neighborhoods that incorporate a full spectrum of housing choices, including workforce housing, compact design, and connections to jobs, transit, services, and education. The Center achieves its mission through a multifaceted program of work that includes conducting research, publishing, convening thought leaders on housing issues, and recognizing best practices that support the mission of the Center.

About Enterprise Community Partners

Enterprise Community Partners works with partners nationwide to build opportunity. We create and advocate for affordable homes in thriving communities linked to jobs, good schools, health care services, and transportation. We lend funds, finance development, and manage and build affordable housing while shaping new strategies, solutions, and policy. Over more than 30 years, Enterprise has created 300,000 homes, invested nearly $14 billion, and touched millions of lives.

About Enterprise Policy Development and Research

The Enterprise Public Policy team works with members of the U.S. Congress, the Obama administration, community development organizations, and other stakeholders to safeguard, expand, and improve housing and community development initiatives that support low- and moderate-income households. The Policy Development and Research division provides thought leadership and data-backed recommendations to influence housing and community development policy, addressing both emerging policy issues and long-term needs.

Acknowledgments

The project team appreciates the input and participation of the nearly 200 individuals engaged as part of this research. A complete list of the research participants is included in an appendix of this report. We also acknowledge the ongoing efforts of the ULI District Councils and Enterprise Market Offices to support this project.

Project Advisory Group

Enterprise and the Terwilliger Center thank the members of the project advisory group for their insights throughout the research and writing process:

Douglas Abbey
Chairman
Swift Real Estate Partners

Dara Kovel
Chief Housing Officer
Connecticut Housing Finance Authority

Chuck Laven
President
Forsyth Street Advisors

Ron Moelis
CEO and Chairman
L + M Development Partners

Cynthia Parker
President and CEO
BRIDGE Housing Corporation

Nancy Rase
President and CEO
Homes for America

J. Ronald Terwilliger
Chairman Emeritus
Trammell Crow Residential

Project Sponsors

Enterprise and the Terwilliger Center acknowledge the generous funding support for the research provided by Douglas Abbey, chairman, Swift Real Estate Partners, through the ULI Foundation, and Ron Moelis, CEO and chairman, L + M Development Partners.

About the Authors

Andrew Jakabovics is the senior director for policy development and research at Enterprise Community Partners.

Prior to joining Enterprise, he served as senior policy adviser to the Assistant Secretary for Policy Development and Research at the U.S. Department of Housing and Urban Development (HUD), where he provided policy recommendations and analysis to the Assistant Secretary, Secretary, and other senior staff both within HUD and across agencies. His primary focus was on housing finance reform, with a particular eye toward issues of access and affordability. In addition, he devoted attention to foreclosure prevention through improving opportunities for modifications and to mitigating foreclosure impacts on neighborhoods and communities.

Prior to joining HUD, Jakabovics served as associate director for housing and economics at the Center for American Progress, where he worked on housing, household debt, higher education, and other issues related to sustaining and growing the middle class. Jakabovics has appeared frequently in the media, primarily for his research, analysis, and policy solutions to the mortgage crisis, the housing finance system, and housing affordability for renters and owners.

Lynn M. Ross, AICP, is the executive director of the ULI Terwilliger Center for Housing at the Urban Land Institute in Washington, D.C. Ross joined ULI in 2012 and is responsible for managing the strategic direction of the Center and for implementing a multifaceted program of work that furthers the development of mixed-income, mixed-use communities and a full spectrum of housing affordable to all.

From 2007 to 2011, Ross was with the National Housing Conference (NHC) and the Center for Housing Policy (CHP), where she was the director of state and local initiatives before being named as the chief operating officer.

Prior to relocating to Washington, D.C., Ross was with the American Planning Association (APA) in Chicago from 2002 to 2007, where she served as the manager of the Planning Advisory Service, managing a staff of six planners and support staff in providing customized planning research to more than 1,200 subscribing agencies in addition to serving as the assistant program director for the annual New Directors Institute and the staff liaison for APA's diversity initiative.

Ross began her career as an independent contractor with the consulting and training firm of Henry Moore Building Communities Inc., where she focused on neighborhood planning, citizen engagement, and program evaluation.

A certified planner, Ross holds a master's of regional planning from Cornell University and a bachelor of science in community and regional planning from Iowa State University. She serves on the editorial advisory board for Housing Policy Debate and the advisory committee for the National Initiative on Mixed-Income Communities.

Molly Simpson is program manager of the ULI Terwilliger Center for Housing. Simpson joined ULI in 2012 and is responsible for developing and implementing educational and research programs related to housing policy and practice, including the Center's publications, webinars, forums, and awards program.

Prior to joining ULI, Simpson was a graduate intern at the U.S. Department of Housing and Urban Development for the Office of Sustainable Housing and Communities, where she supported the Sustainable Housing Initiative, focusing on promoting green, healthy, and energy-efficient affordable housing. She has also worked in sustainable and health-based community development as a consultant to federal clients including the U.S. Environmental Protection Agency and U.S. Centers for Disease Control and Prevention.

Through her role as a consultant, Simpson provided support for several national convenings and served as coordinator for a national network of environmental health capacity-building grantees.

Simpson is currently pursuing a master's degree in sustainable urban planning from the George Washington University and holds a BA in environmental studies with concentrations in political studies and economics from Bard College.

Michael Spotts is a senior policy analyst for Enterprise Community Partners. He joined the public policy team in August 2009. In his position at Enterprise, he conducts research and analysis of affordable housing and community development policies, and manages Enterprise's federal transit-oriented development policy activities.

He serves as vice chair of the Arlington County (Virginia) Affordable Housing Study working group, a member of the county's Community Development Citizen's Advisory Committee, and a member of the board of directors for the Arlington Partnership for Affordable Housing.

Prior experience in the community development field includes work with the Housing Assistance Council, Sustainable Pittsburgh, Allegheny County (Pennsylvania) Economic Development, and the Rural Local Initiatives Support Corporation.

Spotts graduated with a master's of science in public policy and management from the Heinz College at Carnegie Mellon University. He graduated summa cum laude from Dickinson College in 2006, and received a post-baccalaureate certificate in community and economic development from the Pennsylvania State University in 2008.

Contents

Introduction

THE NEED FOR AFFORDABLE rental housing is on the rise. According to *The State of the Nation's Housing 2013*, as of 2011 there were 12.1 million extremely low-income renters, an increase of 2.5 million since 2007.[1] Furthermore, there is a growing body of evidence that the demand for rental housing is growing and that the trend will continue as those under 35 years old form households of their own.[2]

Despite the increasing need, the supply of rental housing is generally not keeping up. According to the National Multi Housing Council, some 300,000 new apartments are needed to meet demand annually, but just 130,000 units were built in 2011.[3] The gap in supply is even more

Tapestry, New York, New York

dramatic when specifically examining affordable rental housing. In 2011, there were just 6.8 million housing units affordable to extremely low-income renters—some 135,000 fewer units than in 2007, a shortfall of 5.3 million units.[4]

In an era of growing demand and declining government financial support for affordable rental housing, it is more important than ever to deliver affordable housing effectively as possible. Bending the cost curve will enable developers to deliver additional affordable rental homes and help jurisdictions provide more housing choices, meet the growing need for affordable rentals, and ensure that individuals and families across a range of incomes have a place to call home within the community. Bending the cost curve will also allow for the most efficient use of what are increasingly scarce public funding sources.

Why Lowering Cost Matters

The delivery of affordable housing is shaped by a number of procedures, regulations, and policies instituted at all levels of the system and at all points in the development process—each with associated costs. Development costs may be dictated by site constraints, design elements, local land use and zoning restrictions, building codes, delays in the development process, efforts to reduce long-term operating costs, and the affordable housing finance system.

Most affordable housing developments rely on multiple funding streams, both equity and debt, each of which carries its own set of requirements and compliance costs. While there may be some alignment of affordable housing land use regulations, financing tools, or programs, far too often developers must seek a complex series of approvals or obtain waivers to bring a development to fruition. This process alone can introduce costs through delays to the development timeline as well as additional uncertainty and risk, which, in addition to regulatory barriers, can also increase costs.

Moreover, developers of affordable housing are often tasked with providing a variety of amenities and services to create opportunities for and improve the lives of residents. Although developers strive to meet a variety of community goals and foster the development of high-quality affordable housing, these criteria tied to amenities and services increase hard, soft, and ongoing compliance costs.

The question of how to lower the cost of developing long-term affordable rental housing has important financial and policy implications. As public funding sources come under threat—in efforts to reduce government expenditures or simplify the tax code—it becomes increasingly necessary to identify opportunities to lower the cost of providing affordable homes.

How the Research Process Worked

While a rich literature on regulatory barriers to affordability exists, much of that literature focuses on specific elements of constraint related to land use and zoning, process delays, and building codes.[5] However, relatively little work has been done to examine how all of these issues, along with financing, interact with and affect affordable housing development. In response to this gap in the literature, Enterprise Community Partners and the Urban Land Institute's Terwilliger Center for Housing launched a joint research effort not only to examine the various factors affecting the cost of developing affordable rental housing, but also to explore possible solutions. It is also important to note that while the Low Income Housing Tax Credit (housing credit) is a critical production tool for affordable rental housing, this research effort examines a broader set of cost challenges and solutions for affordable rental housing development and preservation not exclusive to housing credit support.

Funding for the initiative, launched in September 2012, was provided by Douglas Abbey, chairman, Swift Real Estate Partners, through the ULI Foundation, and Ron Moelis, CEO and chairman, L + M Development Partners. The first phase of work involved our research team convening a series of roundtable discussions in five cities—Chicago, Denver, Los Angeles, New York City, and San Francisco—to explore the question of cost with sensitivity to how the issue varies by market. As part of

the second phase of work, additional interviews were held with an array of practitioners, developers, financiers, and policy makers in five additional markets: Boston, Houston, Minneapolis, Pittsburgh, and Seattle.

As a result of these conversations and other analyses, Enterprise and the Terwilliger Center identified several elements as common drivers of costs in the development of affordable rental housing. These cost drivers were discussed at a high level in an initial report released in last year titled *Bending the Cost Curve on Affordable Rental Development: Understanding the Drivers of Cost.*[6]

Throughout this effort, the research team engaged with nearly 200 key stakeholders representing both weak and strong markets, different population sizes and geographies, and a range of economic and policy environments. The input of these stakeholders was invaluable, particularly as the project team moved to the next phase of the work, which involved identifying best practices and new ideas for solutions to bending the cost curve.

About This Report

Bending the Cost Curve: Solutions to Expand the Supply of Affordable Rentals represents the culmination of over a year of research.[7] This report is organized into two main sections addressing the following questions:

1. What drives costs and why?

2. What are the recommended actions?

This report greatly expands on our earlier publication by providing more detail on the cost drivers, including how those drivers vary by market. In addition, this report offers a detailed set of recommended actions to bend the cost curve with the goal of moving toward a more efficient and lower-cost affordable rental housing delivery system.

These recommended actions apply to actors at the federal, state, and local levels of the housing industry landscape. Whether you are a developer (private or nonprofit), public official, housing finance agency, financier, or advocate, this series of recommendations is intended to arm you with actionable ideas and to stimulate dialogue on this important issue.

What Drives Cost and Why?

IN ORDER TO BUILD a more cost-effective affordable housing delivery system, it is important to identify the factors that contribute to the cost of developing affordable units. Conversations with practitioners throughout the country yielded a significant list of cost drivers. These elements vary by market, project type, and funding source. While some cost drivers are unique to the affordable housing sector, others are experienced by all developers trying to work in a given jurisdiction. This report will identify the following most commonly cited cost drivers and discuss their impact and applicability:

■ Project Scale

■ Project Design and Construction

■ Finance and Underwriting

■ Program and Investor Requirements

■ State and Local Regulations

Project Scale

While a significant portion of upfront cost is directly related to the size and scale of the development, some costs—such as land costs, design costs, legal expenses, and funding application fees—are fixed or only partially correlated to the number of units in a development. In the case of land prices, sellers and brokers often assume that a property will be developed to maximum density at market rates when determining asking prices. These fixed costs make smaller developments (particularly those developed at less than the density allowed by existing zoning and land use codes) less economical on a per-unit basis. Therefore, in some circumstances, per-unit project costs could be reduced by removing the barriers to larger projects.

To build additional units, a developer could use a larger lot or develop an existing site more intensively. While the former method can bring some economies of scale, land and soft costs may increase as a result. A better method

of achieving greater cost-effectiveness may be to develop more units on a given site through increased lot coverage, greater building height, or the construction of smaller units.

However, there are often significant barriers to increasing the number of units built on a given site, including the following: a lack of renter demand for additional units; requirements on density, size, amenities, or design features imposed by jurisdictions or funders; and inadequate funding to cover the incremental increase in total development costs. It should also be noted that additional density does not necessarily lead to lower costs. For example, larger developments may require a shift from wood-frame to more expensive steel construction. Alternatively, a development might be built in phases, thus increasing soft costs.

Project Design and Construction

While reducing the cost of affordable housing development is an important goal, it is important to recognize that savings should not come at the expense of quality. When affordable housing is poorly designed, unattractive, and unsafe, it will fail to meet the goal of providing decent shelter for low- and moderate-income individuals and families.

The importance of high-quality design and construction has been proven over the years through failures (such as the high-rise public housing properties that have required expensive redevelopment) and successes (including mixed-income developments and Low Income Housing Tax Credit developments). Furthermore, many developers intend to own and operate an affordable housing development in perpetuity, whereas comparable market-rate developers might operate under a shorter time horizon. Therefore, higher upfront costs may be economical if the measures improve the long-term viability of the development. Some developers have begun to design and build with greater attention to life-cycle costs.

There are policy, financial, and regulatory barriers to controlling design and construction costs:

■ **Community concerns.** Project designs may need to incorporate certain elements to comply with regulatory requirements, combat community opposition, or meet other policy goals.

■ **Site selection.** Given limited financial resources and a protracted development time frame (in which community opposition may play a significant role), many developers have difficulty locating appropriate sites for affordable housing development. In some cases, affordable developers secure property from the public sector, often redeveloping disinvested infill sites as part of a comprehensive redevelopment plan and at the behest of the locality. As a result, affordable developments may be built on more challenging sites than market-rate developments. When these developments use public resources, developers are often also held to higher standards for environmental remediation.

■ **Price of construction labor.** This is highly market-specific, based on factors including the strength of the market, the level of workforce unionization, the types of projects being built, and the sources of financing, which may impose requirement such as Davis-Bacon prevailing wage scales.[8]

■ **State and local regulations.** Regulations may prohibit innovative building techniques or require standards that exceed codes. Examples include construction models that incorporate manufactured, modular, and panelized housing. Factory-based work can yield savings based on economies of scale in material purchases and the ability to work in a controlled environment, among other factors. While these methods are generally associated with single-family homes, prefabrication is being increasingly used in the multifamily sector, including a 32-story residential tower in Brooklyn, New York, and a 25-story dormitory in the United Kingdom.[9]

Finally, certain industry practices influence costs. Many developers use customized designs for each development, which can be expensive and time-intensive. Developers can often achieve economies of scale by using

Masonvale, Fairfax, Virginia

TORTI GALLAS & PARTNERS INC.

standardized designs and products throughout their own portfolio. Furthermore, the repetition of standardized design and construction could help identify inefficiencies in the process, which could potentially lead to lower costs. However, those who want to reuse designs may encounter several roadblocks depending on the sources of financing and the jurisdiction in which the development is being built.

■ **Design requests from neighborhood groups.** Once again, the opinions of the surrounding neighborhood matter. Communities often want specialization, and developers should be very sensitive about how the scale and aesthetics of the development fit into the fabric of the neighborhood. To address these concerns, developers must often deviate from standardization.

■ **Adapting to the site.** Infill projects and non-standardized sites can create layout challenges. In these cases, replication of design could be inefficient if it takes away from appropriate site analysis.

■ **Jurisdictional fragmentation.** Developers working in multiple municipalities may have difficulty replicating designs, as each jurisdiction often has different codes, standards, and regulations.

Finance and Underwriting

Real estate development is fundamentally shaped by the sources of capital available. For market-rate residential and commercial developments, both investors and developers generally share the common and (comparatively) simple goal of profit maximization. The financing process is more complicated for affordable housing developments. By targeting lower-income households, the developer is reducing or eliminating opportunities for the same level of profit as in a market-rate development in order to provide a benefit to the community. The reduced ability to earn a profit has several implications:

◼ **Investors who are purely yield-driven are less likely to participate in the affordable housing market.** While this loss of capital availability is partially offset by public, nonprofit, and mission-driven actors, the decrease in the number of investors in the marketplace gives those who do participate more power to dictate terms.

◼ **Affordable housing developments tend to be much more complicated.** While some lending institutions will provide conventional financing for affordable developments, developers must balance these sources with lower-cost capital from investors and public agencies that have motivations beyond profits. As a result, developers may be forced to structure the deal around the terms and goals of the funder in addition to the needs of the marketplace. Furthermore, developers must often assemble multiple layers of funding for a given deal given the limited availability of affordable housing capital.

Capital Availability

In general, market-rate deals enjoy more flexible financing than affordable housing deals. Market-rate developers can raise capital for the overall company or a portfolio of properties and then deploy it quickly. Investors are taking risk based on the overall financial health of the company or a pool of deals, rather than each individual deal. This gives investors and developers more flexibility to adapt to changing market demands and cost pressures.

Affordable housing developments, on the other hand, are generally financed with a mix of public and private capital tied to the specific development or jurisdiction. The requirements of public programs and the investors who participate in them influence the types of developments that get built. The affordable housing community has adapted its development model to fit these requirements. It is difficult to change the framework in which affordable housing developers operate, since doing so requires changes to laws, regulations, developer practices, and investor expectations.

The lack of capital availability and flexibility prevents developers from undertaking certain financing structures and development types, which has significant implications for cost control. For example:

◼ **Affordable housing finance is mostly project-based.** Developers must identify properties, begin scoping out a deal, and then start to assemble financing. This creates delays and increases costs. Entity- or portfolio-level capital is rare, but if such financing were available, developers could quickly and strategically deploy this capital when opportunities arise.

◼ **Financing is scarce for the acquisition of multifamily developments needing little to no rehabilitation.** Affordable housing developers without flexible capital are at a disadvantage in competing for these properties, especially in hot markets. In addition, funders—public, private, and nonprofit—can add requirements and regulations that decrease the cost-effectiveness of these investments. If public subsidies are used to make the purchase, the presence of existing tenants who earn more than the subsidy sources' income restrictions could create compliance challenges and/or lead to evictions.

◼ **Financing is often difficult to access or more costly for smaller multifamily projects.** According to 2009 American Housing Survey data, 79 percent of multifamily renter households (excluding renters who live in single-family homes) live in buildings with fewer than 50 units.[10] Origination, underwriting, servicing, and asset management costs generally do not vary by deal size, and thus account for a proportionally higher percentage of costs in smaller deals.[11] This results in higher costs for developers and lower yields for investors. In addition, small loans are often difficult to securitize, so the availability of capital is highly dependent on portfolio lending.[12] However, small multifamily development and preservation is crucial to the affordable housing market overall. Much of this stock is affordable (with or without subsidy). Fannie Mae estimates that 86 percent of its small multifamily loan portfolio is affordable to households at or below 100 percent of area median income.[13] Furthermore, a significant portion of this stock is aging and in need of capital repairs; over half of small rental buildings are more than 30 years old.[14]

- **Capital is often unavailable or difficult to use for developments that incorporate innovative building types or construction methods.** This includes accessory dwelling units (ADUs)[15] and prefabricated structures, which can reduce the per-unit development cost of a project.

- **Mixed-income developments often struggle to obtain financing and often face additional hurdles.** These developments can contribute to economic diversity, community revitalization, and enhanced resident economic mobility. In some scenarios, rents from market-rate units can cross-subsidize affordable units. However, financing these deals can be difficult, as many investors work exclusively with market-rate or affordable developments. Within the financial institutions that finance both of these types of development, affordable and market-rate lending may occur in different departments that may not be accustomed to coordinating, which can add complexity and uncertainty to the deal. Regulatory-related costs and requirements can also disrupt the return structure of the market-rate portion of a mixed-income development. When public funds and/or land are used for mixed-income development, public requirements sometimes end up applying to the entire development, making market-rate more expensive than in a fully unsubsidized development. Finally, project feasibility depends on the strength of the market.

Mixed-income developments can work well in high-cost, urban markets. However, in weaker markets, mixed-income developments must be of higher quality and must be very well located to attract market-rate tenants, whose higher incomes provide them with a wider range of housing choices. These factors can increase costs, which sometimes offset the added revenue from market-rate units and make these deals less profitable.

Deal Structure

Affordable housing development and the acquisition and major rehabilitation of existing housing are generally financed with a combination of debt and equity. The amount of debt a development can carry is based on the amount of income that can be generated by tenants' rental payments. As these rents are set at levels affordable to low- and moderate-income households, the resulting revenue is insufficient to finance the full cost of development through debt alone. Consequently, developers must seek equity investors. The Low Income Housing Tax Credit program is the primary source of equity for affordable multifamily developments, providing capital for more than 100,000 apartments each year and 2.4 million apartments since its creation in 1986.[16] State housing finance agencies (HFAs) award housing credits to developers, and investors purchase those credits to offset tax liabilities, thus providing the equity for the development of affordable homes. Any remaining financing gaps are filled with a combination of sources that can include grants and soft loans.

Unlike other types of real estate developers, affordable housing developers are generally unable to earn returns from either rent or increases in property values. Subsidy programs limit the amount of rent that can be charged to tenants, limiting cash flow. In addition, many affordable housing developers intend to keep their properties affordable for extended periods of time (or in perpetuity) and do not sell the property and earn capital gains. Therefore, their main source of compensation is the developer fee, which is built into the overall deal structure and often counted as an upfront cost. Without these fees, developers would not have the resources to assemble and operate affordable housing investments.

The specific structure of an affordable housing development is often dictated by the particular funding sources that are used. Many of the characteristics of a typical investment directly or indirectly lead to increased costs, including:

■ **Tax credit allocations.** In applying for housing credits, a developer generally submits a funding application with a proposed budget that enumerates project costs. Successful applications will receive a funding allocation based on this budget. This structure reduces the direct incentive to lower costs beyond the HFA cost control standards. In addition, allocations are made early in a process that can take several years to complete. When projecting the budget, developers have an incentive to hedge against the risk of cost inflation and overruns by increasing their upfront figures, since opportunities for a revised allocation are limited. Once the allocations are made, there is little incentive for developers to use less than the full allocation. Equity investors base decisions on the expectation that they will use the full allocation, and therefore in many circumstances any excess funds are used on project upgrades, rather than in a reduction in housing credit equity. While this increases the cost of development, well-designed upgrades will efficiently extend the building's useful life.

■ **Fees.** Many project fees—including developer fees, architecture fees, and legal fees, among others—are based on a percentage of total development costs. This structure reduces the incentive to decrease development costs.

■ **Risk.** Since profit margins are lower for affordable deals, lenders and equity investors have an increased incentive to minimize their risk profile, leading to tighter underwriting standards. Risk aversion can also lead to a preference for a narrow range of development types. This risk aversion has positive and negative aspects. Conservative underwriting can lead to better financial performance. However, conservative underwriting can lead to higher upfront costs (often in the form of higher reserve levels) and limit a developer's ability to undertake innovative deals and development types that may prove to be less costly overall.

■ **Capital reserves.** Developers must set aside a portion of funding for reserves, which are used to cover construction cost overruns, shortfalls in operations funding, a loss of public subsidy, or ongoing maintenance needs. Adequate reserves are necessary because affordable developments operate on thinner margins overall, limiting the cash flow available to deal with problems that may arise. However, investor risk aversion can lead to greater reserve requirements, driving upfront capital costs higher.

By design, the housing credit does not provide enough capital to finance the entire development, and developers must seek out other sources of financing. Since most housing credit developments reach households at lower incomes than basic housing credit restrictions, subsidized public financing is often needed for a portion of the development costs.[17] Furthermore, regulations governing some public funding sources mandate or provide incentives for obtaining additional or "matching" sources of financing. The resulting "layered finance" structure significantly influences costs in the following ways:

■ **Additional paperwork, fees, and due diligence expenses.** Incorporating multiple sources of funding requires specialized consultants and duplicative professionals (attorneys, accountants, etc.).

■ **Barriers to entry.** Deal complexity can narrow the range of developers and professionals to those with the capacity and experience to balance multiple funding sources. The scarcity of capital for affordable housing development creates robust competition that often results in funding being directed to established high-capacity developers and professionals. These developers generally produce affordable homes efficiently. However, deal complexity and the competitive marketplace can create barriers to entry for startup or smaller developers and professionals who may be able to bring innovative practices or effectively fill market niches.

■ **Increased complexity and longer timelines.** More complex deals take longer to assemble, which increases both soft costs and land holding costs. Financing and project details may need to be reworked as time goes by as a result of changing circumstances. Interest rates for various sources of financing may change, as can the price at which investors will buy housing credits. For example, in particularly strong markets such as Houston, affordable housing developers must compete with a robust market-rate sector for subcontractor services. This competition is compounded by ongoing competition with the oil and gas industry for labor. Construction companies may require a premium to agree to work under the more drawn-out (and sometimes uncertain) affordable housing development timeline.

■ **Compliance issues.** Developers must generally comply with multiple (sometimes conflicting) standards and regulations, which drives up complexity and costs. In some circumstances, a developer may be required to conduct the same due diligence items, such as appraisals, reviews, and inspections, separately for each funding source.

■ **Project phasing.** Developers may be forced to split larger developments into phases as separate deals as a consequence of limited funding and the requirements of multiple financing sources. Phasing may be necessary in some circumstances given developer capacity, rental market conditions, and a desire to minimize displacement when redeveloping existing housing. However, numerous costs are associated with project phasing, including soft costs that are incurred for each phase, such as developer, application, design, engineering, legal, and professional fees. In addition, the more extensive timeline increases land holding costs when phased land acquisition is not feasible.

Program and Investor Requirements

Investors and public funding programs can also influence costs based on the specific terms under which funding is made available, including regulations, program requirements, and timing.

First, funder requirements can increase hard costs by imposing specific design and construction standards, though these requirements are also commonly included in municipal building codes and zoning requirements. For

The Kalahari, New York, New York

example, some funding programs and investors institute rehabilitation minimums for developments involving the recapitalization of multifamily housing. The rationale behind these minimums is that investors want to ensure that the property will not encounter deferred maintenance within a few years of rehabilitation. If the property deteriorates, it becomes a greater financial risk. Therefore, many investors prefer to incur more costs in a project upfront to ensure that the property is of lasting, high quality. While these minimums may serve as a barrier to lower upfront costs, they would constitute money well spent if the useful life of the building is extended. Other examples of specific funder and investor requirements affecting hard costs are parking minimums, unit size minimums, storage standards, and amenity requirements.

Funders also influence costs by the timing and methods in which funds are distributed. A notable example is the process through which housing credits are allocated. State HFAs hold annual competitions for housing credits and then developers who receive an award sell those credits to investors through a process called syndication. HFAs determine which developments get funded through their qualified allocation plans (QAPs), which set minimum standards and provide point-based criteria for meeting state priorities. As competition for housing credits is strong in most states, HFAs must balance multiple priorities from a large number of applicants, and the application review process can be lengthy.

These time delays can have significant cost implications, most notably in securing sites and contractor services. Since most affordable housing developments rely on the developer's ability to obtain housing credits, many developers do not complete the site purchase until they receive the allocation. As a result, purchase prices must at times be increased to compensate the seller for the uncertainty and the extended length of time to close the deal. In circumstances when developers do have full site control/ownership prior to the allocation process, they incur holding costs while the housing credit application is under review. The same principle applies to identifying the rest of the development team—contractors and other professionals require a premium to compensate for the uncertain timing.

HFAs also frequently revise the standards and incentives in their QAPs. While examination and improvement are important, they often create a steeper learning curve as developers must adapt to frequent changes. A lack of QAP consistency can also narrow the field of developers, as those who are less experienced with the program may not be able to react as swiftly and effectively to QAP changes. Developers must also comply with other funding timelines. The funding application cycles for secondary financing do not always align with the QAP review timing, further adding to time and costs.

In addition, many research participants stated that there are significant challenges to using tax-exempt private activity bonds, which provide the debt financing for deals that use 4 percent housing credits. First, the interest rates on bond financing are not always competitive with other types of debt, particularly FHA loans. However, in order to be eligible for 4 percent credits, at least 50 percent of eligible land and building costs must be financed by tax-exempt bonds and developers do not have the flexibility to use more competitive sources of debt financing.[18] To comply with this requirement while obtaining more competitive long-term financing, developers sometimes use tax-exempt bonds (incurring all the associated costs), only to repay those bonds after construction completion with a more optimal source of takeout financing.[19] In the meantime, the developer is paying the higher interest rate on the bond financing, driving up costs further.

Incentives to Meet Other Policy Goals

While market-rate developments are primarily assessed according to financial viability, affordable housing developments—particularly those funded through the housing credit program—must compete for funds and are assessed against a variety of social policy standards. The amount of financing available for affordable housing is insufficient to meet demand. Therefore, minimum standards and scoring incentives in QAPs (as well as other funding programs) drive what gets built, as developers compete to meet these standards and design better-scoring projects. While many of these goals are desirable, meeting them can increase hard, soft, and ongoing compliance costs. The following standards and incentives were cited by research participants as having a notable effect on development costs:

■ **Site-specific incentives.** Some state HFAs offer location-specific incentives for projects near transit, in infill locations, or in targeted community revitalization areas, among others. In some cases, these sites can be more expensive—for example, there may be price premiums for transit-served properties. In others—such as infill locations—the site requires significant demolition, remediation, or preparatory work. In addition, the incentives themselves can increase the cost of the property—knowing that the QAP is creating demand for a certain site type, sellers/brokers often increase their asking price.

■ **Commercial space.** In an effort to promote mixed-use development and broader economic growth in a neighborhood, some QAPs (as well as state and local regulations) include incentives or requirements for including on-site commercial space. Affordable housing developers may not have experience in the commercial market; this learning curve can increase costs. It also is often difficult to finance the commercial space, as the projected income often cannot be borrowed against without preleasing the space. In addition, in many cases the requirement for commercial space exceeds the amount that the market can support. Preleasing is particularly difficult in previously disinvested areas, where the project is intended to be a catalyst for further development. These spaces often take time to fill and can have higher vacancy and delinquency risk when compared with national retailers. Vacant commercial space can have a negative impact on the curb appeal of a project, causing spillover effects to the residential portion of the development. When commercial activity does eventually improve in a community as a result of initial reinvestment by the affordable housing sector, subsequent private market participants stand to benefit from the initial housing investment and risk-taking.

- **Community engagement.** Some HFAs give priority to developments that can demonstrate community support. This can put developments that are facing significant not-in-my-backyard (NIMBY) opposition at a significant disadvantage, without regard to the quality of and need for the development. In these circumstances, the developer may be forced to adopt lower densities or make design changes that are not optimal for the development, thereby increasing costs.

- **Match and leverage requirements.** Many QAPs include a minimum match, a leverage requirement, or additional incentive points for exceeding a given standard. To improve competitiveness, some developers may add features in order to pursue additional funds and enhance the leverage score.

- **Other incentives or requirements.** These include historic preservation rules and mandatory amenities such as community rooms, computer labs, and green space.

Green Building and Energy Efficiency

Green building and energy efficiency requirements and incentives constituted the most widely discussed policy goals throughout the research process. Many HFAs have incorporated environmental sustainability into their minimum requirements or added incentive points for meeting performance standards or obtaining a third-party green certification. While green building and sustainable development practices may add capital cost upfront, there is significant potential for ongoing cost savings in the multifamily building sector as well as in other program and policy areas.[20] Estimates of potential gas and electricity consumption savings reach 28 to 29 percent, with savings of up to $9.2 billion in 2011 energy prices.[21] While not every requirement or technique is cost-effective or desirable, evaluations of existing green building measures confirm that well-designed and properly implemented measures can indeed yield significant financial savings. A recent analysis of developments that met Enterprise's Green Communities Criteria achieved lifetime utility cost savings of $3,709 per unit, compared with incremental costs of $3,546 per unit.[22] There are, however, several barriers to achieving the full potential of green building–related cost savings, including:

- **Underwriting.** For a number of reasons, the financial community does not always accept the projected savings when underwriting a deal. These reasons include a lack of familiarity with green building practices, projected payback periods, and whether there is the ability to recapture utility savings for efficiency improvements, particularly in developments that have tenant-paid utilities.

- **Waivers.** Developers sometimes have difficulty receiving agency waivers or adjustments to utility allowances (or other regulations) necessary to recoup cost savings from efficiency investments.

- **Other requirements.** HFAs, governments, and funders sometimes require overly specific measures that may not be cost-effective given the specific project context (for example, requiring individual metering for all units in a senior/supportive housing development).

Incentives for Cost Control

While many QAPs and funding competitions include incentives that drive up costs, a significant number also explicitly include cost-control elements. When designed correctly, cost-control requirements and incentives can serve as a counterweight to other factors that might drive up expenditures, pushing developers to find more efficient methods of achieving those goals. However, poorly designed cost controls can result in a "race to the bottom" in terms of quality and create barriers to certain developments, such as developments that serve families or vulnerable populations. In addition, inaccurately calculated cost caps can even lead to increased costs, as developers and contractors sometimes bid up to the maximum allowable level.

State and Local Regulations

The state and local regulatory framework can have a notable effect on the supply of housing and the cost of development.[23] However, unlike affordable housing financing and program requirements, these factors often affect both market-rate and affordable developments, although in practice the effects are not always equal.

Many state and local regulations and fees have reasonable justifications, including environmental protection and ensuring adequate infrastructure. Growth management policies that allow for denser development within a municipality or region can lead to increased housing supply, and possibly increased affordability.[24] However, other regulations are inefficient at best and discriminatory at worst. Land costs and entitlement and permitting fees can create a substantial cost floor, before a developer even breaks ground, regardless of the developer's efficiency or the project type.[25] As a result of these higher baseline costs, the ability of market-rate housing to reach lower income levels is limited and affordable housing subsidies result in fewer units.

Impact Fees and Entitlements

Most jurisdictions impose a number of conditions before allowing developers to proceed with construction. Existing zoning codes and land use regulations set restrictions on the type and size of developments that can be built on a specific parcel. Developments that fall within those parameters are generally considered "by-right," and can generally proceed without extensive review and approval. Proposed developments that do not fall within this framework must receive the necessary variances and entitlements in order to proceed, which can add delays and costs. In addition, jurisdictions generally impose either direct requirements, to develop or improve the infrastructure surrounding the development, or impact fees, which are used to fund infrastructure and service improvement across the jurisdiction.

In many cases, these requirements are necessary to sustainably manage growth, and developers should pay a fair share for the general upkeep and maintenance of the community. However, inefficiencies in the process can inhibit affordability for the following reasons:

- **Excessive fees and requirements exclude some development.** Impact fees and infrastructure development requirements can be excessive and are sometimes instituted to prohibit affordable housing development, or are enacted in lieu of politically controversial tax increases.

- **Limits on by-right development can prohibit development.** Jurisdictions often put narrow limits on by-right development, in an effort to exert greater control over the types of projects that are built and address community concerns.

- **Flat impact fees are regressive.** Flat impact fees that are not scaled based on unit type or size are regressive, imposing higher costs on smaller projects that may actually have less impact.

- **Unpredictable time frames can increase costs.** The extended time frames and unpredictability associated with the zoning, permitting, and entitlement process can increase both hard and soft costs.

- **Community opposition can inhibit a development.** In many jurisdictions, community stakeholders have one or several opportunities to provide feedback on proposed development projects before they are allowed to proceed. This process can be invaluable for obtaining insights into the neighborhood and to gaining stakeholder buy-in for affordable rental developments. While this process is critically important, it can also lead to increased costs due to time delays or negotiated additions that may or may not enhance the development. When poorly managed, the community engagement process can also be unnecessarily confrontational and strong opposition can lead to the cancellation of the entire development.

- **When developing outside the urban footprint, developers in some jurisdictions have to pay the full cost to extend infrastructure.** With the new infrastructure in place, other developers may follow and build at much lower expense. Such a structure may be useful in urban areas attempting to control sprawl and encourage infill development. However, this can create a significant barrier to affordable housing in rural areas.

Regulations Affecting Project Type

Aside from direct fees and process-related delays, the state and local regulatory framework can influence building types and design, as well as the number of units built.

- **Parking minimums were the most noted barrier over the course of our research.** In some cases, such as in rural markets or in car-dependent communities, it is appropriate to provide large amounts of parking based on market demand. However, large amounts of parking are not always necessary, particularly in areas well served by transit.[26] At the jurisdictional level, parking minimums can decrease the overall supply of housing, discourage certain development types, and increase rents.[27] These effects are also felt by individual developments. Parking requirements increase construction-related hard costs. In addition, dedication of large amounts of land for parking reduces the number of affordable units that can be built and drives up per-unit costs. The cost of parking is especially high in areas where land values are high. One report estimates that a typical parking space in San Francisco adds $25,000 to $50,000 in construction costs for new housing.[28] Developers can still accommodate greater density by incorporating structured parking, but such projects have significantly higher construction costs than those with surface parking. This space may be economically unproductive to the developer if parking minimums exceed the amount needed in the market. When the developer assesses optional fees to defray the cost of parking construction, any insufficient demand would hurt the development's financial performance. If parking construction is financed with housing credit equity, the developer may not charge optional fees. Instead, the cost of parking must be included as part of the tenant's rental payment. Since rent levels are restricted, the developer's ability to recoup the cost of construction

of extraneous parking spaces required by local parking minimums is limited.

- **Jurisdictions can also directly influence the types of projects that can be built through density requirements, height maximums, and size minimums.** Zoning codes can also restrict the locations in which affordable housing can be developed, and may require the incorporation of commercial space into residential development.

- **Some jurisdictions also ban or make it difficult to build specific types of projects.** Group homes, micro-units,[29] and ADUs often face challenges if they are not by-right project types.

Regulations Affecting Hard Costs

Jurisdictions can also impose regulations or restrictions that have a direct impact on site preparation and construction costs.

- **Building codes.** These codes often include accessibility requirements, historic preservation protocols, and energy- and/or water-efficiency standards. Codes may even dictate the specific type and size of amenities that must be incorporated into the project, provisions that may put cost-restrained affordable developments at a disadvantage.

- **Rehabilitation standards.** Similarly, many jurisdictions require that major rehabilitation projects be brought up to current code for new construction. This can lead to significant increases in costs, or make rehabilitation projects cost-prohibitive. This problem can be avoided by adopting separate rehabilitation codes.

- **Site selection.** Jurisdictions can have an impact on hard costs by influencing the type of sites that affordable housing developers can use. Many deals are driven by land purchases from the public sector, where the jurisdiction identifies land for affordable housing development, often as part of a broader community revitalization strategy. Many sites require costly environmental remediation or other site preparation challenges.

Regulations Regarding Public Procurement and Development Team Selection

As previously discussed, the timing and choice of development team members can have a significant impact on costs. The efficiency of the development team is affected by marketplace competition, familiarity with regulations and program requirements, and the ability to value-engineer early in the development process, among other factors. Several federal, state, and local rules affect who can participate as part of the development team and their compensation levels, directly affecting the project budget:

■ **Qualified contractor regulations.** In an effort to ensure that public spending goes toward qualified entities, jurisdictions sometimes create approved vendor lists. While this may prevent lesser-qualified or lower-capacity professionals and subcontractors from receiving public funds, it can also decrease competition and result in higher costs.

■ **Procurement methods.** Some jurisdictions and funding programs (at the federal, state, and local levels) require public, open bidding processes for the selection of subcontractors. These restrictions are in place to prevent procurement-related improprieties. However, these regulations can delay or prevent the value-engineering process.

■ **Procurement preferences.** Jurisdictions may influence the development process to meet other social goals, including but not limited to increasing diversity among public contractors. These preferences/requirements include local hiring, minority- and woman-owned business enterprises (MBEs/WBEs), HUD Section 3 (hiring preferences for low-income workers), and setasides for nonprofit entities.

■ **Wage rate regulations.** Prevailing wage rules, including federal Davis-Bacon standards, can have a significant impact on costs, depending on the labor market in which the project is being built. These standards often require construction workers and trade professionals to be compensated at or near union-level pay rates. This increases costs, which jurisdictions must balance against the social goals of the measure. Setting aside the direct impact of these measures on costs, there are additional challenges in how these policies

are implemented that can further increase labor costs. Residential rates are generally lower than commercial rates. However, in some circumstances shelter-based developments are classified as commercial (either as a result of building size or the inclusion of a significant commercial component in mixed-use developments) and therefore must use higher rates. In addition, if there are not enough residential contractors in an area to determine the regulated wage, commercial construction rates are used, which can increase costs.

Impact of Regulatory Complexity

Each of the aforementioned regulatory barriers can increase the cost of housing preservation and development generally. When all the applicable regulations are taken together, the combined effect can exacerbate the cost impact, especially for affordable housing, where the developer must also meet the multiple program and financing requirements discussed earlier. Developers could better plan for and mitigate the costs of these regulations if the overall framework is simplified, explicit, and straightforward. Unfortunately, this is not always the case:

■ **Jurisdictional fragmentation can lead to significant costs to developers, as they must meet the different standards and codes of each entity.** This factor applies when developers work in multiple municipalities and when they apply for funding/approvals at different levels of government (i.e., local, state, and federal). Requirements and incentives do not always align and are often difficult to reconcile. For example, a state funding program may prioritize developments with a larger number of smaller units, while the local jurisdiction may prefer family-sized units. In addition, funding rounds often lack coordination, extending the development timeline.

■ **Jurisdictions often negotiate with developers over the terms that the project will need to meet to receive necessary permits, variances, and entitlements.** While this process can result in a mutually beneficial resolution, efficiency is sacrificed when developers cannot anticipate the specific standards that the development will need to meet. This process can also lead to last-minute changes that further drive up costs.

What Are the Recommended Actions?

BENDING THE COST CURVE is a complex challenge that varies across markets. Based on the research and interviews conducted as part of this analysis, Enterprise Community Partners and the ULI Terwilliger Center for Housing developed a set of specific, actionable recommendations for lowering the cost of affordable rental housing delivery. The recommendations fall into six broad categories:

1. Promote cost-effectiveness through consolidation, coordination, and simplification.

2. Remove barriers to reducing construction costs and delays.

3. Facilitate a more efficient deal assembly and development timeline.

4. Improve and align incentives.

5. Improve the flexibility of existing sources of financing and create new financial products to better meet needs.

6. Support the development and dissemination of information and best practices.

The remainder of this report will delve into each category and provide details for each recommendation.

1. Promote Cost-Effectiveness through Consolidation, Coordination, and Simplification.

The affordable housing delivery system consists of a diverse range of stakeholder groups, each with its own goals, priorities, and timelines. Rarely are these interests coordinated in a systematic way. However, doing so would result in a simplified, more streamlined system with shorter development timelines and lower costs. The following recommendations focus on eliminating duplication, reducing complexity, and enhancing efficiency throughout the affordable housing delivery system.

Coordinate and consolidate monitoring and due diligence activities. For most developments, each funder and regulatory agency conducts its own due diligence for the deal and ensures compliance with its rules and regulations. This "layered financing" can thus lead to significant duplication, including but not limited to forms, legal documents, and inspections. Financiers and regulatory bodies should coordinate to eliminate overlap in the underwriting, due diligence, and ongoing monitoring processes to the greatest extent possible. This collaboration can take several forms, including developing common forms and protocols for a given region, delegating authority to a lead agency, and deal-by-deal negotiations to reconcile standards and paperwork.

One example is the MassDocs system spearheaded by the Massachusetts Housing Partnership, a statewide public nonprofit organization. MassDocs is a unified loan-closing document system for affordable housing.[30] MassDocs is intended to eliminate duplicative paperwork and legal expenses by combining the loan documentation for each subordinate funding source. The process is completed using an online automatic document assembly system. In the unlikely event of a default, these subordinate lenders are in a joint position (proportionate to loan size) to recoup any assets that remain after all senior debts are repaid. All developments receiving a state subsidy or a federal subsidy passed through to the state must use this system.[31]

While innovations that promote greater coordination, even incrementally, among financiers are important, other models exist that could take this principle to its logical extension. Many market-rate projects are financed through a "participation structure," in which one actor provides the initial financing in full and takes responsibility for all underwriting and due diligence. This actor then "sells" participating stakes to other lenders and investors. Adopting or piloting this model for affordable housing could potentially lead to significant cost reductions. This structure creates a "one-stop shop" for the developer and shifts the burden of assembling multiple layers of financing to the lead financier. This could significantly shorten the deal assembly timeline and limit associated land holding costs, reduce compliance burden, and decrease soft costs associated with layered financing. This model would not be without challenges, however. The lead financier would bear the upfront risk while it found additional investors and lenders and may charge for that risk. Participating investors would need to develop a sufficient level of trust that the lead financier's level of due diligence is sufficient. However, these challenges and risks could be offset by the increased financial viability of the development that results from the aforementioned cost reductions.

Consolidate and coordinate competitive funding competitions. States and localities can help streamline the deal assembly process either by combining the competitions/application cycles for multiple funding sources into a single process, or by coordinating the timelines of separate funding processes. This type of coordination can happen at several levels:

■ Within a jurisdiction by combining federal and state pass-through/block grant funds with local sources;

■ Between the state and local levels;

■ Between jurisdictions within a larger region; and

■ Between government sources and philanthropic funders.

Examples of such coordinated funding competitions exist in a variety of markets. Pennsylvania has a single competitive funding program and application for its loan and housing credit programs.[32] Minnesota has a unified request for proposals that consolidates soft funding from state and large philanthropic lenders.[33]

Once funding is awarded, participating funders and jurisdictions should also consider coordinating the monitoring requirements for the various funding sources into a single report. Though this might require extra time to be spent for upfront negotiating of the requirements and standards of this report, such coordination would reduce ongoing compliance and operating costs.

One potential drawback to a once-per-year funding competition is that if a project application is not ready at the time of the competition, it must wait an entire year to apply, adding delays and costs.

Improve and coordinate codes, zoning, and regulation. Urban regions include multiple jurisdictions of varying size and each with their own regulatory framework. This can create inefficiencies for developers who work across municipal lines. Costs associated with jurisdictional fragmentation can be reduced by ensuring that relevant building codes, zoning procedures, regulations, and planning processes are coordinated to the greatest extent feasible. This model of coordination is more commonly found with regional plans, but similar principles could be applied at the state or county level or where regional governance is already in place. For instance, the metropolitan government of Nashville and Davidson, County, Tennessee, has a unified code that addresses land use, building, and safety regulations for the entire region.[34] When evaluating codes, jurisdictions should also ensure that they are up-to-date and do not require obsolete or nonstandard products and techniques, or add any excessive requirements that can raise costs.

Streamline HUD financing. According to research participants, HUD financing could be improved by coordinating application and approval timelines and by reducing the number of approvals and forms required from different parts of the agency. At present, HUD is undergoing a restructuring initiative with the goal of streamlining and improving its internal operations, including a reorganization of its field office resources.[35] However, this restructuring plan is not explicit about how these changes will affect the financing application process. Regardless of the outcome of that process, there are other actions HUD can take to facilitate greater efficiency in the deal assembly process:

■ Provide a single underwriter for each deal, potentially tied to the HUD Multifamily Office consolidations. Alternatively, underwriters can be tied to relationships with a set of originators and developers, rather than by geography.

■ Provide greater consistency and set more accurate expectations for the length of time it takes to move through the application/underwriting process. This will allow developers to better time their applications, reducing delays or extra costs to extend rate locks.

2. Remove Barriers to Reducing Construction Costs and Delays.

Jurisdictions can help lower costs by eliminating barriers to timely and efficient affordable housing development. This research identified several common regulatory processes that could be altered at the jurisdictional level. These changes will reduce costs and delays, and may also encourage innovation in design and construction.

Implement smart parking requirements. Parking standards should be carefully evaluated based on the needs of residents and the surrounding land use. Especially in urban infill developments near transit, parking minimums may be substantially reduced or eliminated entirely. Examples of "smart parking" codes for transit-accessible locations can be found in many cities including areas of metropolitan Boston, San Francisco, and Seattle, where parking maximums have been set or shared parking has been established, serving more than one use on site.[36]

Review unit size and amenity requirements. Unit size and amenity requirements should also be evaluated to ensure they meet the needs of the people they are intended to serve, while avoiding excess. Adjusting these requirements may reduce per-unit costs, increase density, and allow developments to increase the number of affordable units available. Some cities, including San Francisco, Seattle, and New York, have also started to allow for micro-units, which are often targeted to individuals more interested in affordable, well-located urban living than large unit size.[37]

Make rehabilitation easier. Many jurisdictions require that substantial rehabilitation projects be brought up to code for current new construction. These stringent requirements can make rehabilitation cost-prohibitive. For existing buildings, separate rehabilitation codes should be adopted. These codes should include requirements for structural integrity, occupant safety, and energy efficiency.

Fire Clay Lofts, Denver, Colorado

A special rehabilitation code has been adopted in the state of New Jersey and is among the first comprehensive set of code requirements for existing buildings.[38] These special rehabilitation codes allow buildings to be rehabbed and repurposed without sacrificing affordability.

Improve development team coordination. Central to successful cost control is early and frequent coordination between the developer and members of the development team, including engineers and architects. Some jurisdictions and funding programs require public, open bidding for the selection of subcontractors. These public procurement processes can impede the ability of the development team, including the project manager, to collaborate early and begin the design and value-engineering process. Jurisdictions should remove barriers in the public procurement process to encourage the development team to work together throughout the design and construction phase.

Support innovative building techniques. Jurisdictions should also examine whether their existing regulatory and zoning requirements discourage innovative project types and building techniques, such as micro-units and prefabricated housing. For example, there is significant interest in construction models that incorporate modular, panelized, or manufactured housing. Organizations such as NextStep, a Kentucky-based network of nonprofit homebuilders working to replace the last 2 million inefficient pre-HUD Code mobile homes in the United States with energy-efficient manufactured homes, are facilitating partnerships between the factory-built housing industry and the affordable housing development community. These products offer opportunities for cost savings and architectural innovation. To facilitate these innovations, jurisdictions should review their codes and zoning policies and work to remove barriers. If removing barriers jurisdiction-wide is not feasible initially, approving small-scale pilot projects can be useful to test these innovations and build a case for changes.

3. Facilitate a More Efficient Deal Assembly and Development Timeline.

In addition to changes to streamline the financing assembly process, municipalities, states, and public funders should address regulatory barriers and create incentives to streamline the development process and reduce time-related costs.

Eliminate zoning barriers to by-right housing development. Municipalities can facilitate more efficient development time frames and reduce costs by enabling more by-right development. This can be accomplished by relaxing restrictions related to density, building height, unit size, and parking minimums, thereby freeing developers from the need to seek waivers, variances, or rezoning. Building and zoning codes should also allow for diverse building types and techniques, including but not limited to group homes, micro-units, factory-built housing, and ADUs. Flexibility can also be achieved through compact/cluster site plans and transfer of density rights. Jurisdictions should provide clarity around any fees that may be assessed and/or developer responsibilities. This will improve efficiency by allowing developers to plan accordingly from the beginning of the development process.

Create clarity and structure in the public engagement process. Jurisdictions should revisit their public engagement processes and requirements to ensure that developments are not unnecessarily delayed by

NIMBY opposition, but also receive the many benefits of community input. While there is no single example to point to as the best practice, successful engagement efforts typically involve clarity in both the procedures and the time frame expected for the developers and the community. However, firm time limits without exceptions may not be conducive in every scenario. Such a policy could result in a development being rejected outright rather than being given the opportunity to work through complex issues. The Institute for Local Government recommends that the following three components be present in an effective public participation strategy for affordable housing: (1) resolve uncertainty early in the process with a well-designed process and clear, timely communications; (2) deal with different points of view in the presentation of developments, particularly those that are controversial; and (3) validate participation by ensuring that public views are welcome and respected.[39]

In addition to process clarity, public engagement efforts should employ multiple engagement techniques including public hearings, focus groups, social media, and design charrettes.[40] Using a mix of techniques, in concert with deliberative outreach to a broad diversity of community stakeholders, creates a structure for meaningful input within the process while minimizing the chances for a single meeting to be dominated by a single perspective that may lead to delays.

Adopt state policies to streamline local development. States have the ability to ensure that local jurisdictions provide opportunities for multifamily and affordable housing development. Some states monitor and provide approval for general land use plans, and can use that process to ensure that zoning is in place to accommodate reasonable density. Other states, such as Massachusetts and Connecticut, have adopted policies that allow affordable housing development by-right throughout the state. Though there are many caveats, both states have regulations that allow developers of affordable housing to build at greater density in municipalities where less than 10 percent of the housing stock is designated affordable.[41] This supports the creation of affordable housing across the state, particularly in localities that have a prominent affordability gap. Another option is to make some state funding sources contingent on the adoption of policies that facilitate affordable and multifamily housing development. In developing such policies, states should also avoid policies and regulations that make it easy for a local jurisdiction to "veto" affordable housing development.

Promote QAP consistency. HFAs have the flexibility to amend their QAPs to advance the state's goals and to adapt to market-specific conditions. This flexibility also provides opportunities for experimentation and innovation. However, frequent changes to the QAP can lead to inefficiencies as developers must adapt to the new framework. HFAs should promote consistency by limiting the frequency of changes to the greatest extent feasible; provide specific notice to developers in advance of any significant changes; ensure that developers have sufficient lead time to analyze the changes and adjust accordingly; and provide technical assistance to developers to ensure compliance.

Adopt efficient deadlines for deal assembly and project development. Timeliness is crucial to cost control. In addition to the aforementioned measures to streamline the deal assembly and QAP process, state HFAs can adopt deadlines that require deals to close in a specific number of days. While some flexibility is likely necessary to account for extraordinary circumstances, a deadline could possibly compel developers and financiers to advance through the deal assembly and underwriting/ approval process more quickly. HFAs should also examine their placed-in-service deadline policies, particularly in states where climate is a major factor in the development timeline. While shorter development times may be less expensive in general, increased costs can be incurred when the construction process must be accelerated to complete development before the onset of adverse weather conditions.

4. Improve and Align Incentives.

There are roles for policy makers and financiers at the federal, state, and local levels to improve the incentives and to better align the numerous funding streams, timelines, and approvals needed to develop affordable rental housing. While savings can be achieved by creating financial and regulatory incentives for cost control, it is also important to ensure that quality is maintained and that hard-to-reach populations can still be served.

Evaluate life-cycle cost considerations in the underwriting process. In determining financial viability and the level of reserves that are necessary, underwriters must identify the time horizon in which the development must be operational. In many cases, an assumption is made that the development will need to be recapitalized after 15 years. Yet the life of most buildings is much longer. If the field were to underwrite based on life-cycle costs with a lengthier useful life of the property, it is likely to increase upfront costs—more durable construction materials would be used and reserve levels would need to be increased. However, this could yield significant industry-wide cost savings if it decreases operating costs and the frequency of recapitalization and rehabilitation in the future. An analysis of property-level data by the Center for Housing Policy and National Housing Conference suggests that this underwriting model could be successful.[42] A substantial amount of existing affordable housing could be physically and financially viable for up to 50 years if the properties had complete access to cash flow and refinancing proceeds or with modest additional investment at the time of development. The study also found that the cost savings from avoiding recapitalization outweigh this additional upfront investment.

Create incentives for green building and energy-efficient design. During the course of this research, green building and energy-efficient design requirements and incentives were frequently discussed policy goals that were seen as both essential to producing high-quality, durable affordable rental housing and prevalent drivers of development costs. Though green building measures can add to upfront development costs, a life-cycle cost analysis will identify efficiency measures that have the most compelling payback periods. When determining green building standards, regulators and financiers should focus on efficiency measures that yield significant savings over time. Moreover, these measures should be subjected to careful cost-benefit analysis.

Likewise, for new construction, when requiring that an affordable housing development meet green certification, a consistent set of criteria should be used to reduce

The Hayes at Railroad Square, Haverhill, Massachusetts

compliance costs by streamlining the certification process. For rehabilitation projects, minimum standards can be set that require meeting a specific target, allowing the developer to meet that standard through a variety of potential pathways in the most efficient and cost-effective way possible.[43]

Provide local incentives for affordable housing development. There are multiple opportunities for jurisdictions to offer programs and policies that create and strengthen the incentives to produce affordable rental housing. These include:

■ **Targeting local subsidies toward land acquisition.** Particularly in strong markets, acquiring land in areas that are optimal for affordable housing development— near employment hubs and transit-accessible—can be a barrier to affordable housing development. Jurisdictions can support affordable housing by providing subsidies for land acquisition. Subsidies should be carefully coordinated and funds should be released quickly to allow for timely site control and to condense the predevelopment timeline.

■ **Offering property tax abatements for affordable housing during the development phase.** These abatements provide subsidy during the development phase and reduce soft costs. Portland, Oregon, offers a range of tax abatement programs designed to promote residential development near transit stations, rental housing rehabilitation, and nonprofit ownership of affordable rental homes.[44] Philadelphia offers a residential development property tax abatement equal to 100 percent of the value of the improvements beginning the month after the building permit is issued.[45] The term of the abatement is up to 30 months or until the property is sold, transferred, or occupied.

■ **Adopting impact fee waivers or smart impact fees.** Fee waivers can dramatically reduce predevelopment costs. So-called smart impact fees can be instituted for affordable housing development, whereby smaller unit sizes receive reduced impact fees that scale by number of bedrooms or anticipated household size. In addition, states can encourage jurisdictions to eliminate barriers to building affordable housing by reducing or even eliminating impact fees where other community goals are being met.

■ **Providing expedited review and permitting for affordable housing developments.** Many jurisdictions have such programs, but they are often contingent on additional fees. This service should be provided at no cost and jurisdictions should set clear and consistent expectations on the review and permitting time frame to minimize predevelopment delays and reduce holding costs. Montgomery County, Maryland, has implemented the Green Tape Program to provide a streamlined and expedited permit process for commercial construction in state-designated enterprise zones and for residential or mixed-use developments that meet certain criteria.[46] To qualify, residential or mixed-use developments must designate at least 20 percent of the total number of housing units for residents with income levels in line with the county's signature moderately priced dwelling unit (MPDU) program.[47] Qualifying developments receive expedited application review and permit processing.

■ **Subsidizing land or infrastructure costs.** Jurisdictions can subsidize the cost of land and infrastructure improvements in exchange for the creation of affordable rental housing on site. This technique, which is especially useful in master-planned communities and planned unit developments, can be coupled with overlay zoning to allow for greater density, relaxed parking requirements, and increased housing diversity.

■ **Creating "first-look" programs when disposing of public land.** Federal, state, and municipal agencies should establish first-look programs to give affordable housing developers right of first refusal for local public land. To ease predevelopment and holding costs, these jurisdictions can also hold land until it is ready for development.

Consider cost in the QAP process. HFAs should implement carefully studied direct incentives or requirements for cost control in the QAP process. Adjusting QAPs to incorporate cost control as a central metric can occur in a variety of ways. While some stakeholders found that using cost caps was an effective way to control development costs, others noted significant challenges with this approach. Poorly designed cost caps can reduce project quality, create barriers to developments serving vulnerable populations or high-cost markets, and lead to increased cost, as developers and contractors sometimes bid up to the maximum allowable level. These challenges underscore the importance of identifying accurate cost thresholds and points of comparison.

An alternative method is to incorporate cost control as a rating factor in the QAP scoring criteria. For example, the Minnesota Housing Finance Agency awards points to the 50 percent of proposals with the lowest costs, adjusted for development type. This "blind bid" approach creates additional competitive pressures to keep costs low. This process supplements Minnesota's analysis of cost reasonableness, which is based on a predictive cost model that uses development cost data from throughout the state.[48]

HFAs could also base competitions on a variety of non-cost-related criteria and disqualify developments that are beyond a cost threshold. They can also revise the QAP process altogether by identifying top priorities and incorporating them into basic standards. A request for proposals could be issued by the HFA and affordable housing developments could compete on a cost basis.

Consider the time frame in which costs are evaluated for the purpose of underwriting. In determining financial viability and the level of reserves that are necessary, underwriters must identify the time horizon in which the project must be operational. In many cases, an assumption is made that the project will need to be recapitalized after 15 years, yet the life of most buildings is much longer. If the field were to underwrite based on life-cycle costs with a lengthier useful life of the property, it is likely to increase upfront costs—more durable construction materials would be used and reserve levels would need to be increased. However, this could yield significant industry-wide cost savings if it decreases operating costs and the frequency of development resyndication and recapitalization.

Remove perverse incentives that can increase costs. A number of perverse incentives are built into the affordable housing delivery system that can increase costs. HFAs and other major project funders should consider the following actions to better align incentives toward cost control.

■ **Reduce the number of expenses calculated as a percentage of total costs.** In assembling a development team, developers and funders should explore alternate compensation models, including set-price contracts and/or fee structures that redirect a share of the cost savings to the contractor/developer. However, such contracts would have to be structured in a way that does not have a negative impact on project quality or penalize projects in higher-cost markets.

■ **Provide flexibility in housing credit allocation amounts.** To prevent the overstatement of costs in project budgets, HFAs can consider offering initial allocations to developments at a lower amount and allow limited flexibility to receive an additional allocation if there are unavoidable cost overruns. The Pennsylvania Housing Finance Agency reserves 5 percent of its annual allocation for developments that have received an initial reservation of housing credits and are seeking additional funding. To be eligible to compete for this setaside, developers must first reinvest an amount equivalent 15 percent of the developer fee to cover the increased costs.[49] This policy limits the incentive for applicants to overstate their initial budget by providing an opportunity to address cost overruns. The developer reinvestment requirement ensures that there is a continued incentive to stay as close to the initial budget as possible.

■ **Create incentives to preserve contingency funds.** For example, if there are unused contingency funds, the developer could be allowed to keep a percentage, with the funder recapturing the remainder.

5. Improve the Flexibility of Existing Sources of Financing and Create New Financial Products to Better Meet Needs.

A number of potential innovations exist that could significantly reduce affordable housing development costs, but they require the availability of sufficient capital for implementation. Given investor risk aversion, wholesale adoption of new techniques is unlikely. However, there are many opportunities to conduct pilots, often involving public/private partnerships, to demonstrate the financial viability of these concepts.

Explore entity-level financial products. Entity-level financing could allow developers to more flexibly and quickly respond to market opportunities, including the acquisition of existing multifamily developments. Entity-level financing would also shorten the development timeline, as developers would not have to delay projects while raising capital. Though examples are rare, some developers have successfully used the real estate investment trust model, and a Pennsylvania developer refinanced multiple properties with a single bond issuance.[50] States and the philanthropic community may consider offering incentives for lenders and equity investors to invest in such products. Such incentives may include interest rate subsidies, risk-sharing agreements, and portfolio- or entity-level tax credits.

In order for this model to be successful on a broader scale, investors would need assurance that the developer has a sufficiently strong balance sheet to carry entity-level debt. A voluntary rating system for developers, similar to the CARS system for Community Development Financial Institutions (CDFIs), could be useful in demonstrating capacity and reducing due diligence complexity.[51] Research from the Housing Partnership Network also suggests that policy changes would be necessary to allow developers to aggregate cash flows from different properties to repay the debt and allow for portfolio-level management.[52]

Facilitate investment in the acquisition of existing multifamily properties. A significant portion of the existing affordable housing stock is in unsubsidized rental properties or subsidized properties with expiring affordability restrictions. These developments often have existing tenants and immediate revenue-generating potential. Acquiring these properties and assembling them into a portfolio can be an effective means of creating affordable housing if the challenges of scattered-site property management can be overcome. Both the Housing Partnership Equity Trust and Community Development Trust have successfully used the real estate investment trust (REIT) structure to facilitate this type of acquisition and portfolio assembly.[53]

While some limited resources exist for the acquisition and rehabilitation of the existing housing stock, increasing capital and regulatory flexibility could make these developments more efficient at a broader scale.

■ **Support acquisition of properties needing little or no rehabilitation.** Many affordable housing finance sources require that acquisition deals also include a rehabilitation component. While many existing properties are older and in need of improvements to extend their useful life, a more flexible funding source could facilitate strategic acquisitions. Funders can also consider providing regulatory flexibility to projects with rehabilitation needs below a specific threshold.

■ **Provide flexibility for properties with existing tenants.** Many existing properties (particularly those without significant rehabilitation needs) will be fully occupied. Most financing sources require that all or most of the tenants in a development meet income standards, which could force displacement of existing over-income tenants. Funders can provide flexibility to developers to defer or temporarily waive income requirements for units rented by income-ineligible households, so that eviction can be avoided—possibly in exchange for an extended overall affordability period. The market-rate rents for these units could be used to support the development's overall finances or to fund deeper income targets for other units. The Connecticut Housing Finance Agency's Market to Affordable Conversion Program gives developers up to 18 months to meet income restrictions in all committed affordable units.[54]

■ **Facilitate financing for smaller deals.** Though more difficult to access and less broadly available than conventional financing for larger buildings, capital for smaller deals does exist, particularly through Fannie Mae and from mission-driven CDFIs. Nearly 70 percent of Fannie Mae's multifamily book by loan count consisted of small loans (under $3 million nationwide or $5 million in high-cost markets) as of the end of 2011.[55]

  ▪ **Ensure market liquidity during government-sponsored enterprise (GSE) reform.** Given the status of the GSEs in government conservatorship following the housing crisis, their future is uncertain. Congress and the White House should ensure that any future reform efforts preserve the GSEs' crucial role in providing liquidity in the multifamily market, including smaller deals in particular.

  ▪ **Create public/private partnerships to provide capital for smaller deals.** In states such as Connecticut, state agencies are partnering with CDFIs, local banks, and the community development industry to provide financing for smaller projects.[56] This collaborative structure combines the access to capital of large state entities with the knowledge and on-the-ground relationships of local actors that are helpful in bringing smaller developments to market in a timely and efficient manner. While some products are geared toward preserving existing affordable housing, others provide financing for market-rate developments that will continue to be affordable for lower-income residents.

Facilitate more efficient use of project reserves.
Experienced affordable housing developers with numerous developments have a significant amount of capital tied up in various reserves. Investors and developers can partner to develop innovative reserve arrangements to reduce upfront costs or to free up resources for the development/preservation of additional units.

■ **Substitute guarantees for a portion of reserves.** Reserve levels can be reduced if a third-party guarantee is available to offset the risk. The fees for these risk guarantees could be scaled to the strength and track record of the developer. State-level entities are well placed to develop these guarantees. The Boston Foundation and the Massachusetts Housing Partnership (MHP) created and now operate the Housing Reserve Assurance Program, designed to free up project reserves.[57] Under this program, developers pay a fee for access to a credit facility, which can be drawn down upon if a development experiences cash flow problems. This allows developers to reduce the amount of operating reserves they must keep for the property.

■ **Allow a portion of reserves to be released over time.** Developers can negotiate agreements that allow for excess project reserves to be released over time if the project performs financially at an agreed-upon level.

■ **Explore opportunities for corporate-level or pooled reserves.** When reserves are project-based, investor risk is more narrowly focused on the viability of that specific deal, whereas portfolio-wide reserves shift risk from the specific development to the developer. Developers could provide a guarantee to investors to cover operating shortfalls, backed by a corporate reserve fund. Investors would require developers to have particularly strong balance sheets and performance histories to compensate for the changed risk profile. Since the investor profile of each deal may vary for a given developer, portfolio-level reserves may be difficult to achieve at first. As an interim step, a developer may be able to pool reserves among the deals within its portfolio that share common investors.

Provide greater flexibility in 4 percent Low Income Housing Tax Credit investments. The 4 percent housing credit is an important source of funding for affordable housing development, particularly for acquisition or rehabilitation. There are several options for making this program more cost-effective:

- **Allow alternate sources of debt financing.** In order to be eligible for 4 percent credits, at least 50 percent of eligible land and building costs must be financed by tax-exempt bonds.[58] As these bonds are sometimes more expensive than other sources of debt, cost savings could be achieved if rules were changed to allow alternate forms of debt to accompany 4 percent housing credits, such as FHA multifamily loans.

- **Allow private placement of bonds or direct bond purchases.** Developers incur the costs associated with mandatory public issuance of tax-exempt bonds. While private placement or direct purchases of tax-exempt bonds are not always less expensive than public issuance, additional flexibility in structuring these investments could lead to savings in certain circumstances.

- **Explore parity trust indentures.** The portion of a bond contract that stipulates the terms and conditions for the transaction is known as a trust indenture. Trust indentures are generally created for each deal, which increases legal costs. This cost can be reduced by developing parity trust indentures, which are standardized versions that would apply to financial transactions with similar characteristics.

6. Support the Development and Dissemination of Information and Best Practices.

The diversity of markets, jurisdictions, government agencies, and developers across the country creates significant opportunities for experimenting with different cost-control measures. Therefore, it is important to share the results of these experiments so that others can learn from both best practices and mistakes.

Create a competition to support innovative practice. At the federal policy level, there are significant opportunities to learn from and reward states and jurisdictions that are effectively tackling the issue of lowering the cost of developing affordable rental housing. Specifically, a federal agency–led competition could reward states that have the most cost-effective affordable housing delivery system with a bonus allocation of housing credits, perhaps as a priority in awarding "national pool" credits. This national competition would both serve as a platform to share cost-control measures and strategies among states, and motivate HFAs and other state and local policy makers, financiers, and developers to more effectively coordinate to reduce costs to win both national recognition and a coveted pool of additional housing credits.

Determine appropriate units of measurement and comparison. Productive policy changes require a foundation of accurate information and data to guide decision making. Total development costs can be a misleading metric that jurisdictions and funders should look beyond when evaluating the cost-effectiveness of affordable housing. A number of other methods exist for evaluating development costs, each with advantages and drawbacks. More research needs to be done on these methods to establish best practice. The most appropriate measure (or combination of measures) may depend on the priorities of the evaluating agency and the market in question.

- **Costs-per-unit** is the most straightforward measure of costs, aside from total development costs. However, this metric fails to account for unit size, number of bedrooms, and other characteristics. Developments in markets with high land costs and those with family and supportive units are at a disadvantage using this measure.

- **Costs-per-square-foot** is another standard comparison. It improves upon costs-per-unit by adjusting for the overall size of the development— larger family units are at less of a disadvantage when this comparison is used. However, this measure does not create an incentive to ensure that building common areas and units are sized efficiently, unless accompanied with an evaluation of overall development costs.

- **Costs-per-bedroom** is another metric that removes the evaluation bias against larger units designed to serve families. Unlike costs-per-square-foot, this measure creates the incentive to be economical in determining the appropriate size for units—all things being equal, a smaller three-bedroom unit will score better than a larger three-bedroom unit. However, this metric has an inherent bias against smaller units, particularly studios and one-bedroom units. This would make it more difficult to develop housing targeted toward single-person households.

- **Cost-per-person-housed** is a rarely used metric, but one that most directly addresses the goal of providing affordable housing. Unlike other metrics that measure outputs (developments, units, etc.), this metric directly addresses the outcome of housing low-income people.[59] Similar to cost-per-bedroom, evaluating on this basis adjusts for the household type being served, and provides an incentive to house residents in the most efficient manner possible. However, this metric is less precise, since occupancy figures must be projected and can change over time.

Evaluators will also need to consider the points of comparison and expenses that are included in the calculation.

- **Evaluate by project type.** Developments can be categorized and compared to others with similar characteristics. For example, Pennsylvania has separate reservations of credits for applications that address senior occupancy, preservation, supportive housing, and community revitalization.[60]

- **Evaluate by market.** Statewide funders can choose to separate funding competitions and QAP evaluations by geographic location. Virginia reviews applications by geographic region, which often correlates with the relative expensiveness of the market.[61] Illinois complements its statewide pool of credits with separate reservations of credits for Chicago and other market types throughout the state.[62] Pennsylvania splits its housing credit allocation into "urban" and "suburban/rural" cycles.[63]

- **Separate out specific costs.** Evaluators can control for a number of factors by removing certain costs from the evaluation. For example, the market type can be partially controlled for by removing land/acquisition costs from the evaluation.

- **Separate the costs of meeting other goals.** As previously discussed, jurisdictions, funders, and programs often use affordable housing as a platform for other policy goals. In communicating and evaluating development costs, it may be helpful to separate the costs of these additional features (such as commercial space and on-site services) to create a more accurate comparison with other developments that do not incorporate these elements.

Build a community of practice. The Terwilliger Center and Enterprise effort to explore ways to bend the cost curve of affordable housing helped to create a platform for a diverse group of developers, financiers, policy makers, and others to share lessons learned and emerging industry standards among peers. As cost drivers can be both market-specific and heavily influenced by federal policy, many research participants noted that a community of practice for information sharing is needed at the local, market, and national levels. National organizations with local affiliates, such as Enterprise's Market Offices and ULI's District Councils, have existing networks of local housing leaders. The affordable housing development community should continue to foster these discussions through existing local and market-based channels. Further research and discussion are needed at the market level, and these outcomes and best practices should be leveraged across a national community of practice.

Create a forum for sharing data and best practices. This research sparked an important dialogue about the need to lower the cost of developing affordable rental housing, at the local, regional, and national scale. Moreover, this research identified a continuing need to have an online platform for the affordable housing community—including developers, financiers, policy makers, and others—to share best practices, emerging strategies, case studies, research, data, and dialogue about how to bend the cost curve toward a more efficient and effective affordable rental housing delivery system. This forum might be hosted by a national research or policy organization or by an academic institution.

Conclusion

THE DEMAND FOR MORE RENTAL HOUSING is real and growing, but supply is not keeping up. The United States is in the midst of a demographic sea change that will also signal major changes in where and how people live.[64] As the nation emerges from the Great Recession and begins to consider what the new landscape can and should look like, understanding the needs and desires of residents becomes that much more critical. Beyond this understanding, the ability of developers to deliver affordable rental units—new or preserved—to the market in greater quantities takes on more urgency. While this report provides a wide-ranging analysis of the affordable housing delivery system, there are three key lessons that can be drawn from this work:

Masonvale, Fairfax, Virginia

TORTI GALLAS & PARTNERS INC.

Lesson 1: The drivers of cost run deep.

Our research clearly demonstrates that the drivers of cost come at all points in the development process and are deeply intertwined. Of course, the degree to which the cost drivers identified through our research apply to specific developments varies by market and there may be other factors that can influence an individual development's costs.

Lesson 2: Collaboration is key to taking action.

This research has also identified a number of recommended actions, existing best practices from a range of communities, and possible next steps to help bend the cost curve. Clearly, mitigating or eliminating key cost drivers will require multiple stakeholders to engage and collaborate on a sustained basis to build a more efficient affordable housing delivery system.

Lesson 3: Leadership is essential.

Implementing our suggested recommendations will take creativity, commitment, and time. Moreover, to truly bend the cost on affordable rental development, leadership will also be required. Why leadership? Bending the cost curve by implementing the suggested recommendations will not be easy; it is essential that this work have true champions within every stakeholder group—developers, public officials, financiers, etc.—to keep the momentum going.

Much progress has been made since the Housing Act of 1937, which first established low-income housing subsidies and the creation public housing, and set a goal of providing "decent, safe, and sanitary housing" for all in America. However, it is clear that there is still much more to do in order to achieve this goal. Our hope is that this report will not only continue the dialogue facilitated through our research effort, but also help spark the type of action, thought leadership, and innovation needed to reshape the housing landscape with more affordable rental housing.

Notes

1. Joint Center for Housing Studies, *The State of the Nation's Housing 2013* (June 2013): www.jchs.harvard.edu/research/state_nations_housing.

2. Bipartisan Policy Center, *Demographic Challenges and Opportunities for U.S. Housing Markets* (March 2012): http://bipartisanpolicy.org/sites/default/files/BPC%20Housing%20Demography.pdf.

3. National Multi Housing Council, *Apartments Work: The Policymaker's Guide to Rental Housing* (April 2013): http://nmhc.files.cms-plus.com/ContentFiles/General/Priorities-Brochure-Web.pdf.

4. Joint Center, *State of the Nation's Housing 2013*.

5. Access the U.S. Department of Housing and Urban Development's Regulatory Barriers Clearinghouse: www.huduser.org/portal/rbc/home.html.

6. Urban Land Institute, *Bending the Cost Curve on Affordable Rental Development: Understanding the Drivers of Cost* (2013): www.uli.org/research/centers-initiatives/terwilliger-center-for-housing/research/cost-of-rental-housing/.

7. The findings in this report are largely based on interviews and conversations conducted as part of the research, unless otherwise indicated in the notes. Sources of specific comments are not identified in the report in order to facilitate candid conversations about difficult topics.

8. Administered by the U.S. Department of Labor, the Davis-Bacon and Related Acts stipulate that laborers and mechanics performing work on federally funded or assisted contracts must be paid "no less than the locally prevailing wages and fringe benefits for corresponding work on similar projects in the area."

The impact of Davis-Bacon varies greatly according to local labor market conditions, including the type of construction projects being undertaken. According to some research participants, problems are created when an area has an insufficient amount of development of a particular type. If there are not enough residential contractors in an area to determine the appropriate Davis-Bacon wage, more expensive commercial wage rates may be used as a proxy, which can lead to a substantial increase in costs.

Information on the Davis-Bacon Act can be found at U.S. Department of Labor—Wage and Hour Division, "Davis-Bacon and Related Acts": accessed December 4, 2013, www.dol.gov/whd/govcontracts/dbra.htm.

9. Anthony Flint, "There's More Than History at Stake for NYC's First Pre-Fab High Rise," The Atlantic Cities website (December 18, 2012): www.theatlanticcities.com/housing/2012/12/theres-more-history-stake-worlds-first-pre-fab-high-rise/4193/.

10. Jamie Woodwell, "The GSEs, FHA and Multifamily—Just the Facts," Mortgage Bankers Association (May 2012): www.mbaa.org/files/Research/IndustryArticles/Woodwell0512.pdf.

11. Fannie Mae, "Fannie Mae's Role in the Small Multifamily Loan Market" (2011): 20, www.fanniemae.com/content/fact_sheet/wpmfloanmkt.pdf.

12. Terri Ludwig, "Housing Finance Reform: Essential Elements of the Multifamily Housing Finance System" (2013): http://1.usa.gov/1c4fXdj.

13. Fannie Mae, "Fannie Mae's Role," 14.

14. Ibid., 18.

15. Accessory dwelling units are defined by HUD as "additional living quarters on single-family lots that are independent of the primary dwelling unit." HUD Office of Policy Development and Research and Sage Computing Inc., "Accessory Dwelling Units: Case Study" (Washington, DC: U.S. Department of Housing and Urban Development, June 2008): www.huduser.org/portal/publications/adu.pdf.

16. National Council of State Housing Agencies, "2012 Questions and Answers on the Housing Credit Program" (2012): www.ncsha.org/resource/2012-qa-housing-credit-program.

17. The housing credit program provides apartments for households earning 60 percent of area median income (AMI) or less. However, 43 percent of households living in housing-credit units are extremely low income (earning no more than 30 percent of AMI), and about 37 percent of households earn between 31 and 50 percent of AMI. Furman Center for Real Estate and Urban Policy, and Moelis Institute for Affordable Housing Policy, "What Can We Learn About the Low-Income Housing Tax Credit Program by Looking at the Tenants?" (New York University, 2012): http://furmancenter.org/files/publications/LIHTC_Final_Policy_Brief_v2.pdf.

18. Beth Mullen, "How to Use Bonds in LIHTC Deals," Affordable Housing Finance (May 1, 2006): www.housingfinance.com/economic-development/how-to-use-bonds-in-lihtc-deals.aspx.

19. Richard Gerwitz, "Four Percent LIHTC Developments Take Advantage of Unusually Low Taxable Mortgage Rates," *Novogradac Journal of Tax Credits* IV, no. XI (November 2013): www.novoco.com/journal/2013/11/news_bond_201311.php.

20. A study from Seattle has shown that residents of buildings that meet green building standards can experience reductions in asthma-related symptoms. Tim K. Takaro, James Krieger, Lin Song, Denise Sharify, and Nancy Beaudet, "The Breathe-Easy Home: The Impact of Asthma-Friendly Home Construction on Clinical Outcomes and Trigger Exposure," *American Journal of Public Health* 101, no. 1 (January 2011): www.enterprisecommunity.com/resources/ResourceDetails?ID=67822.pdf.

While health improvements do not directly lead to cost savings for affordable housing operations, the connection between housing and health can lead to innovative financial partnerships that leverage health-related cost savings to provide additional resources for housing and expand the supply of affordable units. New York is using Medicaid resources to construct nearly 5,000 affordable supportive housing units. Josh Dawsey, "New York State Rethinks Medicaid: Seeks to Relocate Thousands of Low-Income Patients," *Wall Street Journal* (August 2, 2013): http://online.wsj.com/news/articles/SB10001424127887323681904578642182234426580.

21. Benningfield Group Inc., "U.S. Multifamily Energy Efficiency Potential by 2020" (Folsom, CA: The Energy Foundation, October 27, 2009): www.benningfieldgroup.com/docs/Final_MF_EE_Potential_Report_Oct_2009_v2.pdf; and HUD Office of Policy Development and Research, "Quantifying Energy Efficiency in Multifamily Rental Housing," Evidence Matters (Summer 2011): www.huduser.org/portal/periodicals/em/summer11/highlight1.html.

22. Yianice Hernandez and Peter Morris, "Enterprise Green Communities Criteria: Incremental Cost, Measurable Savings Update," Enterprise Community Partners, June 2012.

23. An analysis of Massachusetts communities found that a higher level of restrictive zoning led to less development of multifamily housing, both in absolute terms and relative to the jurisdiction's existing housing stock. Jenny Schuetz, "Land Use Regulation and the Rental Housing Market: A Case Study of Massachusetts Communities" (Cambridge, MA: Harvard Joint Center for Housing Studies, March 1, 2007): www.jchs.harvard.edu/research/publications/land-use-regulation-and-rental-housing-market-case-study-massachusetts.

A HUD analysis of regulatory barriers in single-family housing development found that the average barrier resulted in costs of $11,910 per unit, with aggregate costs of $14.6 billion nationwide in 2004. Though these data do not reflect the costs to multifamily housing, it is illustrative of the high cost of regulatory barriers on housing. U.S. Department of Housing and Urban Development, Partnership for Advancing Technology in Housing, and NAHB Research Center, "Study of Subdivision Requirements as a Regulatory Barrier" (Washington, DC: HUD Office of Policy Development and Research, November 2007): www.huduser.org/publications/commdevl/subdiv_report.html.

24. Arthur C. Nelson, Rolf Pendall, Casey J. Dawkins, and Gerrit J. Knaap, "The Link between Growth Management and Housing Affordability: The Academic Evidence" (Washington, DC: Brookings Institution Center on Urban and Metropolitan Policy, February 2002): www.brookings.edu/research/reports/2002/02/housingaffordability.

25. Research on California's regulatory climate found that housing prices and rental costs were 30 to 50 percent higher in the most regulated cities than those in cities with the least regulation. While this increase is not entirely attributable to the regulatory climate, the analysis showed that the relationship between rents and the amount of regulation was statistically significant. Finally, the study found that each additional regulatory measure reduced the growth in a city's housing stock by 0.3 percentage point. John M. Quigley and Steven Raphael, "Regulation and the High Cost of Housing in California" (Berkeley, CA: University of California, Berkeley, December 2004): 11–12, 17, http://works.bepress.com/john_quigley/40/.

26. Daniel H. Rowe, Dr. Chang-Hee, Christine Bae, and Qing Shen, "Assessing Multifamily Residential Parking Demand and Transit Service," *ITE Journal* (Washington, DC: Institute of Transportation Engineers, December 2010): 20–24.

27. A Los Angeles–based natural experiment showed that when parking requirements are removed, developers provide more housing and less parking. Renters in buildings without on-site parking saved an average of $1,500 per year. Different types of housing were also developed, particularly "housing in older buildings, in previously disinvested areas, and housing marketed toward non-drivers" (though external factors may also have had an influence on these shifts).

Michael Manville, "Parking Requirements as a Barrier to Housing Development: Regulation and Reform in Los Angeles" (Los Angeles: Lewis Center for Regional Policy Studies, Institute of Transportation Studies, UCLA, March 2010): http://lewis.ucla.edu/content/parking-requirements-barrier-housing-development-regulation-and-reform-los-angeles.

28. SPUR, "Reducing Housing Costs by Rethinking Parking Requirements" (June 1, 2006): www.spur.org/publications/library/report/reducing-housing-costs-rethinking-parking-requirements.

29. Micro-units are smaller apartments (sometimes as small as 200 square feet) that are designed to minimize wasted space. While some have self-contained kitchens and bathrooms, others have shared facilities. These apartments are often marketed toward single people and young professionals, especially in high-cost markets. In the context of affordable housing, micro-units can be a solution to providing supportive housing for the formerly homeless and those with special needs. However, many jurisdictions have minimum size and other requirements that prevent these units from being built by-right. Susan Johnston, "Micro Apartments Offer Small Slice of City Living," *US News and World Report*, November 15, 2013, sec. Money—Personal Finance: http://money.usnews.com/money/personal-finance/articles/2013/11/15/micro-apartments-offer-small-slice-of-city-living.

30. For more information on MassDocs, visit https://www.massdocs.com/hdsportal/.

31. Any lender that refuses to use the MassDocs loan documentation would be put in third lien position for repayment in the event of default, only being repaid after all senior and secondary liens are satisfied.

32. Pennsylvania Housing Finance Agency, "Multifamily Housing Application Package and Guidelines": www.phfa.org/developers/developer/housingapplication.aspx.

33. Minnesota Housing Finance Agency, "Minnesota Multifamily Rental Housing Common Application": www.mnhousing.gov/wcs/llite?c=Page&cid=1358905251684&pagename=External%2FPage%2FEXTStandardLayout.

34. For more information on the unified code for the Metro Government of Nashville and Davidson County, visit www.municode.com/library/TN/Metro_Government_of_Nashville_and_Davidson_County.

35. For more information about HUD's Office of Multifamily Housing restructuring plans, see "Transforming for the 21st Century": http://portal.hud.gov/hudportal/HUD?src=/transforming_hud.

36. Metropolitan Area Planning Council, "Maximum Parking Allowances," Boston: www.mapc.org/resources/parking-toolkit/strategies-topic/parking-allowances; Metropolitan Transportation Commission, "Parking Code Guidance: Case Studies and Model Provisions," San Francisco (June 2012): www.mtc.ca.gov/planning/smart_growth/parking/6-12/Parking_Code_Guidance_June_2012.pdf.

37. City of Seattle, "Micro-Housing": https://www.seattle.gov/dpd/codesrules/changestocode/micros/background/default.htm.

38. Rehabilitation Subcode of the Uniform Construction Code, New Jersey Administrative Code Title 5, Chapter 23, Subchapter 6: www.state.nj.us/dca/divisions/codes/codreg/pdf_regs/njac_5_23_6.pdf.

39. Institute for Local Government, "Building Support for Affordable Housing: A Toolbox for California Officials" (July 2007): www.ca-ilg.org/document/building-public-support-affordable-housing-toolbox-california-officials.

40. National League of Cities, "Bright Spots in Community Engagement: Case Studies of U.S. Communities Creating Greater Civic Participation from the Bottom Up" (April 2013): www.nlc.org/Documents/Find%20City%20Solutions/Research%20Innovation/Governance-Civic/BrightSpots-FINAL_4-26.pdf.

41. Massachusetts's 40 B Planning statute "enables local Zoning Boards of Appeals to approve affordable housing developments under flexible rules if at least 20-25% of the units have long-term affordability restrictions." Commonwealth of Massachusetts, "Chapter 40 B Planning": http://www.mass.gov/hed/community/40b-plan/. Connecticut has a law similar to the one in Massachusetts. For more information, see Connecticut Department of Economic and Community Development, Section 8-30g: www.ct.gov/ecd/cwp/view.asp?a=1095&Q=307632&PM=1#g6.

42. Maya Brennan, Amy Deora, Ethan Handelman, Anker Heegaard, Albert Lee, Jeffrey Lubell, and Charlie Wilkins, "Lifecycle Underwriting: Potential Policy and Practical Implications" (Washington, DC: Center for Housing Policy and National Housing Conference, February 2013): www.nhc.org/media/files/LifecycleUnderwriting_PolicyPaper.pdf.

43. At the federal level, an interagency working group, including HUD, the U.S. Department of Agriculture, and the White House Domestic Policy Council, is creating an energy efficiency framework for rental housing that proposes recommendations for energy efficiency requirements in federal rental housing programs for both new construction and rehabilitation. For more information, see Rental Policy Working Group, "Federal Rental Alignment": 23–32, www.huduser.org/portal/aff_rental_hsg/RPWG_Conceptual_Proposals_Fall_2011.pdf.

44. Portland Housing Bureau, "2010–2011 Annual Report: Residential Tax Exemption Programs" (December 2011): http://efiles.portlandoregon.gov/webdrawer.dll/webdrawer/rec/4666006/view/2010-11%20Limited%20Tax%20Exemption%20Annual%20Report.PDF.

45. City of Philadelphia, Pennsylvania, Office of Housing and Community Development: www.phila.gov/ohcd/taxabate.htm.

46. More information on the Montgomery County, Maryland, Green Tape Program can be found at: https://permittingservices.montgomerycountymd.gov/DPS/customerservice/GreenTape.aspx.

47. A detailed explanation of the Montgomery County, Maryland, moderately priced dwelling unit program can be found at: www.montgomerycountymd.gov/DHCA/housing/singlefamily/mpdu/index.html.

48. Minnesota Housing Finance Agency, "2014/2015 Housing Tax Credit Qualified Allocation Plan, Cost Containment Methodology" (2013): http://bit.ly/1gb1i5f.

49. Pennsylvania Housing Finance Agency, "Allocation Plan for Year 2014: Low Income Housing Tax Credit Program" (September 12, 2013): www.phfa.org/forms/multifamily_program_notices/qap/2014_qap_final.pdf.

50. Real estate investment trusts (REITs) are real estate companies modeled after mutual funds in which investors can purchase stock to fund the acquisition and operation of income-generating properties. National

Association of Real Estate Investment Trusts, "What Is a REIT?" REIT.com (2013): www.reit.com/REIT101/WhatisaREIT.aspx.

Housing Development Corporation MidAtlantic in Lancaster, Pennsylvania, refinanced seven housing credit properties with a single bond issue. In doing so, it was able to aggregate seven separate cash flows and save operating expenses by merging seven audit requirements into one.

Housing Partnership Network, "Toward a Housing Policy Reform Agenda" (March 2013): 14.

51. More information on the CARS comprehensive ratings for CDFI investments can be found at http://carsratingsystem.net/. Housing Partnership Network. "Toward a Housing Policy Reform Agenda": 17.

52. The Housing Partnership Network recommends that HUD conduct a portfolio-level management demonstration that would provide the regulatory flexibility necessary to test the model of entity-level finance and management. Housing Partnership Network, "Toward a Housing Policy Reform Agenda": 14–17.

53. Both the Housing Partnership Equity Trust and the Community Development Trust use the REIT model to preserve affordable housing. More information can be found at www.housingpartnership.net/enterprises/equity-trust/ and http://cdt.biz/whatwedo.htm.

54. Under this program, developments must have a minimum of 85 market-rate units. Half the units with committed affordability restrictions must be rented to income-eligible tenants within the first six months. The developer has an additional year to meet the remaining income requirements. More information is available through the Connecticut Housing Finance Agency, www.chfa.org/default.aspx.

55. Fannie Mae, "An Overview of Fannie Mae's Multifamily Mortgage Business" (Washington, DC: Fannie Mae, May 1, 2012): https://www.fanniemae.com/content/fact_sheet/multifamilyoverview.pdf; Fannie Mae, "Fannie Mae's Role."

56. In September 2013, the Connecticut Housing Finance Agency initiated its pilot Small Multifamily Lending Program. Target properties financed have three to 20 units per building. Program objectives include rehabilitating vacant or blighted properties, increasing the affordable housing stock in higher-income geographies, and community revitalization in low- and moderate-income geographies. More information is available at www.chfa.org/About%20Us/Requests%20for%20Proposals/viewer.aspx?id=158.

57. The Boston Foundation and Massachusetts Housing Partnership, "Housing Reserve Assurance Program" (September 10, 2013): www.mhp.net/uploads/resources/rap_term_sheet_faq.pdf.

58. Mullen, "How to Use Bonds in LIHTC Deals."

59. Brian Deppe, "Development Cost Trends in Multifamily Housing" (Minneapolis, MN: Minnesota Housing Finance Agency, August 2013).

60. Pennsylvania Housing Finance, "Allocation Plan."

61. Virginia Housing Development Authority, "The Plan of the Virginia Housing Development Authority for the Allocation of Low-Income Housing Tax Credits," 2013: www.vhda.com/about/Planning-Policy/Pages/LIHTC-QAP.aspx#b.

62. Illinois Housing Development Authority, "2013 Low Income Tax Credit Qualified Allocation Plan" (2013): www.ihda.org/developer/documents/2013QAP_Final.pdf.

63. Pennsylvania Housing Finance, "Allocation Plan."

64. ULI Terwilliger Center for Housing and ULI Infrastructure Initiative, *America in 2013: A ULI Survey of Views on Housing, Transportation, and Community* (2013): www.uli.org/research/centers-initiatives/terwilliger-center-for-housing/research/community-survey/.

Appendix 1: Resources

Resources Related to Why Lowering Development Cost Matters

Enterprise Community Partners. "Innovation for Long-Term Solutions." *Neighborhood Foreclosure Recovery*. Columbia, MD: Enterprise Community Partners. www. enterprisecommunity.com/solutions-and-innovation/ community-revitalization/neighborhood-foreclosure-recovery.

Joint Center for Housing Studies of Harvard University. *America's Rental Housing: Evolving Markets and Needs*. Cambridge, MA: Joint Center for Housing Studies of Harvard University, 2013. http://jchs.harvard.edu/ research/publications/americas-rental-housing-evolving-markets-and-needs.

McIlwain, John. *Housing in America: The Next Decade*. Washington, DC: Urban Land Institute, 2010. www.uli.org/ report/housing-in-america-the-next-decade/.

Minnesota Preservation Plus Initiative. *The Space Between: Realities and Possibilities in Preserving Unsubsidized Affordable Rental Housing*. Minneapolis, MN: Minnesota Preservation Plus Initiative, 2013. www.fhfund.org/_dnld/ reports/Space_Between_Final_June%202013.pdf.

Terwilliger, J. Ronald. *America's Housing Policy—The Missing Piece: Affordable Workforce Rentals*. Washington, DC: Urban Land Institute, 2010. www.uli.org/report/ americas-houisng-policy-the-missing-piece-affordable-workforce-rentals/.

The Mortgage Resolution Fund. Chicago, IL: The Mortgage Resolution Fund. http://mortgageresolutionfund.org/.

Resources Related to Understanding the Drivers of Cost

Center for Housing Policy. *"Don't Put It Here!" Does Affordable Housing Cause Nearby Property Values to Decline?* Insights from Housing Policy Research. Washington, DC: Center for Housing Policy, 2009. www. nhc.org/media/documents/Dontputithere.pdf.

Knaap, Gerrit, Stuart Meck, Terry Moore, Robert Parker. *Zoning as a Barrier to Multifamily Housing Development*. Chicago, IL: APA Planning Advisory Service, 2007.

Manville, Michael, and Donald Shoup. *Parking Requirements as a Barrier to Housing Development: Regulation and Reform in Los Angeles*. Los Angeles, CA: Lewis Center for Regional Policy Studies, Institute of Transportation Studies, UCLA, 2010. http://lewis. ucla.edu/content/parking-requirements-barrier-housing-development-regulation-and-reform-los-angeles.

Schmitz, Adrienne. *Multifamily Housing Development Handbook*. Washington, DC: Urban Land Institute, 2000.

Shoup, Donald. *The High Cost of Free Parking*. Chicago, IL: APA Planners Press, 2005.

ULI Rose Center. Webinar: "Parking Reform: How Parking Innovations Can Encourage Transit- and Pedestrian-Friendly Infill Development." Washington, DC: Urban Land Institute, 2013. www.uli.org/online-learning/rose-center-webinar-parking-reform/.

Resources Related to Specific Recommendations

1. Promote cost-effectiveness through consolidation, coordination, and simplification.

Haughey, Richard. *Getting Density Right: Tools for Creating Vibrant Compact Development.* Washington, D.C.: Urban Land Institute, 2008.

Morris, Marya. *Smart Growth Codes: Model Land-Development Regulations.* Chicago, IL: APA Planning Advisory Service, 2009.

2. Remove barriers to reducing construction costs and delays.

Metropolitan Transportation Commission. "Parking Code Guidance: Case Studies and Model Provisions." San Francisco, CA: Metropolitan Transportation Commission, 2012. www.mtc.ca.gov/planning/smart_growth/parking/6-12/Parking_Code_Guidance_June_2012.pdf.

Schmitz, Adrienne. *Affordable Housing: Designing an American Asset.* Washington, DC: Urban Land Institute, 2005.

Smith, Mary. *Shared Parking.* Washington, DC: Urban Land Institute, 2005.

3. Facilitate a more efficient deal assembly and development timeline.

Lennertz, Bill, and Aarin Lutzenhiser. *The Charrette Handbook: The Essential Guide for Accelerated, Collaborative Community Planning.* Chicago, IL: APA Planners Press, 2006.

4. Improve and align incentives.

Brennan, Maya, Amy Deora, Ethan Handelman, Anker Heegaard, Albert Lee, Jeffrey Lubell, and Charlie Wilkins. *Lifecycle Underwriting: Potential Policy and Practical Implications.* Washington, DC: Center for Housing Policy and National Housing Conference, 2013. www.nhc.org/media/files/LifecycleUnderwriting_PolicyPaper.pdf.

Global Green USA. "Top 20 No- or Low-Cost Green Building Strategies." Santa Monica, CA: Global Green USA. http://globalgreen.org/pdfs/05_twenty_strats.pdf.

Hernandez, Yianice, and Peter Morris. *Enterprise Green Communities Criteria: Incremental Cost, Measurable Savings.* Columbia, MD: Enterprise Green Communities, 2012. www.enterprisecommunity.com/servlet/servlet.FileDownload?file=00P3000000DTXI6EAH.

5. Improve the flexibility of existing sources of financing and create new financial products to better meet needs.

Housing Partnership Network. "Housing Partnership Equity Trust." Boston, MA: Housing Partnership Network. www.housingpartnership.net/enterprises/equity-trust/.

Housing Partnership Network. "Toward a Housing Policy Reform Agenda." Housing Partnership Network, March 2013.

6. Support the development and dissemination of information and best practices.

Deutsche Bank Americas Foundation and Enterprise Community Partners. "Lowering the Cost of Housing Competition." Columbia, MD: Enterprise Community Partners, 2013. www.enterprisecommunity.com/loweringcost.

Appendix II: Research Participants

Douglas Abbey
Swift Real Estate Partners

Olukayode Adetayo
Housing Authority of Cook County, Illinois

Leila Ahmadifar
Affordable Housing Investors Council

Charmaine Atherton
Bank of America

Laura Bailey
Capital One

Mary Kay Bailey
Minnesota Philanthropy Partners

Alma Balonon-Rosen
Enterprise Community Partners

Tara Barauskas
A Community of Friends

Trey Barbour
Trek Development Group

Brian Barnes
Housing Authority of Cook County, Illinois

Vicki Been
NYU Furman Center for Real Estate and
Urban Policy

Manuel Bernal
City of Los Angeles–Los Angeles
Housing Department

Annette Billingsley
Union Bank of California

Andrew Brand
Evergreen Housing

Glenn Brill
FTI Consulting

David Brint
Brinshore Development

Heather Bunn
Rafn Company

Heather Burns
Seattle Office of Housing

Cathy Capone Bennett
ULI Minnesota and Regional Council of
Mayors

Colleen Carey
The Cornerstone Group

Erin Carson
City of San Francisco, California

Felix Ciampa
ULI New York

Gina Ciganik
Aeon

Allison Clark
John D. and Catherine T. MacArthur
Foundation

Jessica Cohen
DESC

Mariam Colon
New York City Department of Housing
Preservation and Development

Michael Costa
Highridge Costa Housing Partners LLC

Mark Curtiss
Massachusetts Housing Partnership

Kevin Daniels
Daniels Development

Lisa Davis
Ford Foundation

Caren Dewar
ULI Minnesota

Kerry Dickson
Related

David Doig
Chicago Neighborhood Initiative

Emily Dorfman
University of North Carolina, Chapel Hill

Tamara Dudukovich
Bridgeway Capital

James Eby
The Community Builders

Laurie Eckhardt
Seattle Office of Housing

Stephen Fairfield
Orchard Community Development
Corporation

Daniel Falcon
McCormack Baron Salazar

Steven Fayne
Citi Community Capital

Frances Ferguson
NeighborWorks America

Hal Ferris
Spectrum Development Solutions LLC

Zach Fox
Harvard University

Terry Freeman
Terry Freeman & Associates LLC

Rich Froehlich
New York City Housing Development
Corporation

Breann Gala
Metropolitan Planning Council

Julie Garver
Innovative Housing Inc.

Bill Gatti
Trek Development Group

Andrew Geer
Enterprise Community Partners

Richard Gerwitz
Citi Community Capital

John Ginocchi
Trek Development Group

Holly Glauser
Pennsylvania Housing Finance Agency

Gail Goldberg
ULI Los Angeles

Ingrid Gould Ellen
NYU Furman Center for Real Estate and
Urban Policy

Kevin Griffith
BRIDGE Housing Corporation

Ron Griffith
Century Housing

Rich Gross
Enterprise Community Partners

Evelyn Guerrero
Hispanic Housing Development
Corporation

Tory Gunsolley
Houston Housing Authority

Holly Haff Muchnok
ULI Pittsburgh

Chip Halbach
Minnesota Housing Partnership

Kathy Head
Keyser Marston Association

Ryan Hettig
Hettig/Kahn Holdings Inc.

Scott Hoekman
Enterprise Community Investments

Matt Hoffman
Enterprise Community Partners

Rick Holliday
Holliday Development

Bill Huang
Pasadena Housing Department

Robin Hughes
Adobe Communities

Amay Indamar
AAI Affordable Housing

Marty Jones
Mass Development

Peter Kaplan
PNC Bank

Victor Karen
City Enterprises

John Keaton
Group Gordon

Matthew Kelly
Phipps Houses

Caroline Kenney
Urban Atlantic

Andrew Knudtsen
Economic & Planning Systems

Rebecca Koepnick
NYU Furman Center for Real Estate and
Urban Policy

Doris Koo
Enterprise Community Partners (Retired)

Dara Kovel
Connecticut Housing Finance Authority

Sarah Krautheim
ULI New York

Karen Lado
Enterprise Community Partners

Katie Lamont
Tenderloin Neighborhood Development
Corporation

Tory Laughlin
Taylor Bellwether Housing

Chuck Laven
Forsyth Street Advisors

Mary Lawler
Avenue Community Development
Corporation

Michael Leccese
ULI Colorado

James Lehnhoff
Metropolitan Council

Duane Leonard
Housing Authority of Snohomish County,
Washington

M.A. Leonard
Enterprise Community Partners

Dora Leong Gallo
A Community of Friends

Sarah Letts
Community Corporation of Santa Monica

Linda Mandolini
Eden Housing

Kelly Mann
ULI Northwest

Janet Masella
Washington State Department of
Commerce/Housing Trust Fund

Dean Matsubayashi
Little Tokyo Service Center Community
Development Corporation

John McIlwain
ULI Terwilliger Center for Housing

Kim McKay
BRIDGE Housing Corporation

Cynthia McSherry
ULI Chicago

Margaret Miller
The John Stewart Company

Ron Moelis
L+M Development Partners

Shannon Moriarty
NYU Furman Center for Real Estate and
Urban Policy

Ehud Mouchly
READI LLC

Eric Muschler
The McKnight Foundation

Ron Nahas
Rafanelli and Nahas

Peter Nichol
CWCapital

Sondra Nielsen
DESC

Otis Odell
PWBS Architects

Shola Olatoye
Enterprise Community Partners

Laurie Olson
Seattle Office of Housing

Katherine O'Regan
NYU Furman Center for Real Estate and
Urban Policy

Don Oshita
Chicago Housing Authority

Peter Pappas
Terwilliger Pappas Multifamily Partners

Eta Paransky
City of Houston Department of Housing
and Community Development

Cynthia Parker
BRIDGE Housing Corporation

John Patterson
Minnesota Housing Finance Agency

Bill Pavao
California Tax Credit Allocation
Committee

Ron Perlmutter
Kadamin Realty Corp.

Chuck Perry
Perry Rose LLC

Beth Pfeifer
The Cornerstone Group

Michael Pitchford
Community Preservation and
Development Corporation

Katie Porter
Capitol Hill Housing

Rick Prahler
Hawaii Housing Finance and
Development Corporation

Leslie Price
Washington State Housing Finance
Commission

Cindy Proctor
Beacon Development

Sean Rae
Trammel Crow Residential

Nancy Rase
Homes for America

Beth Reetz
Metropolitan Council

John Reilly
Fordham Bedford Housing Corporation

Robert Riggs
The Community Preservation
Corporation

Bobby Rivers
Camden Builders

Jason Robertson
Florida Center for Workforce Housing Inc.

Victor Rodriguez
Rodriguez Associates

Adam Rogers
Illinois Housing Development Authority

Hipolito "Paul" Roldan
Hispanic Housing Development
Corporation